NEW DIRECTIONS FOR ADULT AND CONTINUING EDUCATION

Ralph G. Brockett, *University of Tennessee, Knoxville*
EDITOR-IN-CHIEF

Alan B. Knox, *University of Wisconsin, Madison*
CONSULTING EDITOR

Current Perspectives on Administration of Adult Education Programs

Patricia Mulcrone
William Rainey Harper College

EDITOR

Number 60, Winter 1993

JOSSEY-BASS PUBLISHERS
San Francisco

CURRENT PERSPECTIVES ON ADMINISTRATION OF ADULT EDUCATION PROGRAMS
Patricia Mulcrone (ed.)
New Directions for Adult and Continuing Education, no. 60
Ralph G. Brockett, Editor-in-Chief
Alan B. Knox, Consulting Editor

LC 85-644750   ISSN 0195-2242   ISBN 1-55542-714-6

NEW DIRECTIONS FOR ADULT AND CONTINUING EDUCATION is part of The Jossey-Bass Higher and Adult Education Series and is published quarterly by Jossey-Bass Inc., Publishers, 350 Sansome Street, San Francisco, California 94104-1342 (publication number USPS 493-930). Second-class postage paid at San Francisco, California, and at additional mailing offices. POSTMASTER: Send address changes to New Directions for Adult and Continuing Education, Jossey-Bass Inc., Publishers, 350 Sansome Street, San Francisco, California 94104-1342.

SUBSCRIPTIONS for 1993 cost $47.00 for individuals and $62.00 for institutions, agencies, and libraries.

EDITORIAL CORRESPONDENCE should be sent to the Editor-in-Chief, Ralph G. Brockett, Department of Educational Leadership, University of Tennessee, 239 Claxton Addition, Knoxville, Tennessee 37996-3400.

Cover photograph by Wernher Krutein/PHOTOVAULT © 1990.

CONTENTS

EDITOR'S NOTES

The adult and continuing education administrator has always needed to be a manager, director, or coordinator of programs. Besides having expected skills and competencies, the administrator has had to develop enhanced skills, increase leadership responsibilities, and adapt to changing roles, particularly in the last decade. This volume, *Current Perspectives on Administration of Adult Education Programs,* examines some of the developments in the field that have led the administrator to acquire enhanced skills and competencies. In effect, this sourcebook helps to explain how the adult education administrator's official (or unofficial) job description has most likely changed.

The literature to guide the adult education administrator has increased over the last three decades, but it has not yet received sufficient attention in graduate studies and scholarly writings to satisfy practitioners (Knox, 1991). The literature has been primarily in three major categories: management, administration, and leadership, with overlap among the categories. In those works intended primarily for management or administration, entire volumes or specific chapters have dealt with topics such as philosophy and mission, goals and objectives, planning, organization and structure, staffing, budgeting, marketing, and evaluation (Langerman and Smith, 1979; Knowles, 1980; Elias and Merriam, 1980; Strother and Klus, 1982; Knox, 1986; Eble, 1988; Merriam and Cunningham, 1989). Sometimes topics (such as planning, program development, or evaluation) that could be placed in the general categories of management or administration have been given special attention in separate works (Anderson and Ball, 1978; Patton, 1986; Deshler, 1984; Knox and Associates, 1986; Marsick, 1988; Seldin, 1988).

While the category of leadership has also overlapped with management and administration, leadership (or leaders) has received separate and increased attention in the literature. Leadership has been used to describe teachers, counselors, program planners, directors, managers, trainers (developers) of educators, and policy makers (Houle, 1992). Houle reviewed over twenty works on leaders and leadership from 1941 to 1991, of which some of the most recent are by Brookfield (1988), Jarvis and Chadwick (1991), Waldron and Moore (1991), and Brockett (1991). Knox (1991) writes about leadership in a program administration context. Edelson (1992) views leadership within the newer paradigm of the learning organization.

Courtenay (1990) studied adult education administration literature from 1936 to 1989, using the Sork and Buskey (1986) framework for analyzing program development literature. He describes administrative context (such as adult basic education and continuing higher education), level of program (such as community, institutional, or organizational), and literature base (such as opinion, adult education, or nonadult education sources).

The Courtenay study utilized nine administrative functions thought to be necessary in all organizations: philosophy and mission, goals and objectives, planning, organization and structure, leadership, staffing, budgeting, marketing, and evaluation. The greatest frequency of contexts for adult education literature were continuing higher education and generic organizational environments. More than half the literature base has references to nonadult education or integrated (adult and nonadult) sources. The charts indicate that leadership, organizing, and structuring were the administrative functions that appeared most often in the references. Also, the literature analyzed contains few controversies or issues and leans greatly toward practical applications.

The studies confirm that there is not an abundance of literature to guide the adult education administrator, who has had to rely essentially on knowledge gained through practice or literature in related fields. The literature available through 1989 largely has not been within the common sources of adult education, and issues existing in administration have not been examined in print. Research in the last decade has served particular segments (for example, training or higher education) or has fallen into specific categories such as administration and supervision of vocational-technical education, cooperative education, or education for employment. In general, there is a need for more research on administration.

As a contribution to needed literature on adult education administration, in the chapters that follow, eleven professional adult educators discuss some current perspectives regarding enhanced skills and competencies necessary for the adult and continuing education administrator (or manager or leader). In Chapter One, I emphasize the need for the adult education administrator to utilize resources within the unit or parent organization as well as those in the external local and greater community for program development. In Chapter Two, in a historical context, Thomas W. Heaney identifies educational, social, and political issues; professionalization; and the decline of social purpose in adult education. Ernest W. Brewer, in Chapter Three, guides the adult education administrator through the grant writing and implementation processes. Charles G. Ericksen, in Chapter Four, demonstrates how the budget is crucial to the effectiveness and efficiency of an adult education organization.

In Chapter Five, Mary S. Charuhas describes ways in which the adult education administrator can utilize focus groups; task forces; advisory committees, councils, or boards; coalitions; cooperatives; consortia; alliances; subcontracts; partnerships; and planning councils. Dennis Terdy, in Chapter Six, gives some deserved attention to the field of staff development, including preservice and in-service programs. Dennis R. Porter, in Chapter Seven, aims to improve administrative functions through the utilization of technology.

In Chapter Eight, Robert C. Mason emphasizes the importance of preparation for an adult education evaluation. He defines evaluation, identifies purposes, and reviews the Joint Committee on Standards for Educational Evaluation's four major standards for educational evaluation and the newer indicators of quality. In Chapter Nine, Sally Vernon, Lisa B. Lo Parco, and Victoria J. Marsick illustrate new ways of thinking about teaching and learning and raise questions about approaches to accountability. Finally, in Chapter Ten, I discuss the influences of philosophies on administrative practice and project how administrators holding respective philosophies approach management and leadership roles and view instruction and instructors.

Patricia Mulcrone
Editor

References

Anderson, S. B., and Ball, S. The Profession and Practice of Program Evaluation. San Francisco: Jossey-Bass, 1978.

Brockett, R. G. (ed.). Professional Development for Educators of Adults. New Directions for Adult and Continuing Education, no. 51. San Francisco: Jossey-Bass, 1991.

Brookfield, S. D. Training Educators of Adults. New York: Routledge, 1988.

Courtenay, B. C. "An Analysis of Adult Education Administrative Literature, 1936–1989." Adult Education Quarterly, 1990, 40 (2), 63–77.

Deshler, D. (ed.) Evaluation for Program Improvement. New Directions for Continuing Education, no. 24. San Francisco: Jossey-Bass, 1984.

Eble, K. E. The Art of Administration: A Guide for Academic Administrators. San Francisco: Jossey-Bass, 1978.

Edelson, P. J. (ed.). Rethinking Leadership in Adult and Continuing Education. New Directions for Adult and Continuing Education, no. 56. San Francisco: Jossey-Bass, 1992.

Elias, J. L., and Merriam, S. B. Philosophical Foundations of Adult Education. Huntington, N.Y.: Krieger, 1980.

Houle, C. O. The Literature of Adult Education: A Bibliographic Essay. San Francisco: Jossey-Bass, 1992.

Jarvis, P., and Chadwick, A. Training Adult Educators in Western Europe. London: Routledge, 1991.

Knowles, M. S. The Modern Practice of Adult Education: From Pedagogy to Andragogy. Chicago: Follett, 1980.

Knox, A. B. Helping Adults Learn: A Guide to Planning, Implementing, and Conducting Programs. San Francisco: Jossey-Bass, 1986.

Knox, A. B. "Educational Leadership and Program Administration." In J. M. Peters, P. Jarvis, and Associates, Adult Education: Evolution and Achievements in a Developing Field of Study. San Francisco: Jossey-Bass, 1991.

Knox, A. B., and Associates. Developing, Administering, and Evaluating Adult Education. San Francisco: Jossey-Bass, 1980.

Langerman, P. D., and Smith, D. H. Managing Adult and Continuing Education Programs and Staff. Washington, D.C.: National Association for Public Continuing and Adult Education, 1979.

Marsick, V. J. (ed.). Enhancing Staff Development in Diverse Settings. New Directions for Continuing Education, no. 38. San Francisco: Jossey-Bass, 1988.

Merriam, S. B., and Cunningham, P. M. Handbook of Adult and Continuing Education. San Francisco: Jossey-Bass, 1989.

Patton, M. Q. Utilization-Focused Evaluation. (2nd ed.) Newbury Park, Calif.: Sage, 1986.

Seldin, P. Evaluating and Developing Administrative Performance: A Practical Guide for Academic Leaders. San Francisco: Jossey-Bass, 1988.

Sork, T. J., and Buskey, J. H. "A Descriptive and Evaluative Analysis of Program Planning Literature, 1950–1983." Adult Education Quarterly, 1986, 36 (2), 86–96.

Strother, G. B., and Klus, J. P. Administration of Continuing Education. Belmont, Calif.: Wadsworth, 1982.

Waldron, M. W., and Moore, G.A.B. Helping Adults Learn: Course Planning for Adult Learners. Toronto: Thompson Educational Publishing, 1991.

PATRICIA MULCRONE is professor and chair of the Adult Educational Development Department at William Rainey Harper College, Palatine, Illinois.

The utilization of human and material resources internal and external to the adult education program is explored as a means to develop programs, and successful cooperative programs are highlighted.

Developing Internal and External Program Resources

Patricia Mulcrone

The adult and continuing education professional today must be extremely resourceful in order to meet community needs and promote program growth and development. In this chapter, I provide a rationale for resource development, explore external resources, describe methods to promote program development, give examples of successful cooperative ventures, and raise future issues related to program development. (See discussion of partnerships in Chapter Two, adequate resources in Chapter Three, and corporate resources in Chapter Nine.)

Rationale for Resource Development

What are resources? Resources are nonhuman (financial and nonfinancial) or human, and they are internal or external to the adult education unit or the parent organization. Financial resources are actual dollars, matching dollars (according to a set formula), or in-kind contributions. In-kind contributions are equivalent dollar amounts based on a percentage of salary to reflect time allocated to a project, volunteer assistance, or free use of nonfinancial resources such as facilities or space, equipment, or materials (Dahl, 1986; Knox, 1991).

Human resources are members of an administrator's own staff or others who can contribute expertise in given areas. For example, if one needed to design a workshop on outcomes-based assessment, internal resources could be members of an institutional curriculum committee, philosophy faculty, testing and measurement staff, counseling staff responsible for the student intake process, and selected students whose educational outcomes are assessed. External assessment resources could be university faculty, state board of education staff who collect data on student educational gains, or independent consultants.

Why does the adult and continuing education administrator need to develop other resources? Dahl (1986, p. 179) gave as a rationale for interagency collaboration the unique resources, expansion of financial base, and additional flexibility of both financial and nonfinancial resources. Another reason is that there have been observed changes in the increasing numbers and types of agencies involved in new or expanded aspects of adult education. These changes have placed increased demands on the adult education administrator for the delivery of services and for the sharing of expertise.

The adult education administrator could consider the resources of any of these in program development: universities; community, technical, or community colleges; public schools; business and industry; the military; libraries; museums; park districts; correctional facilities; cooperative extension; churches; community-based organizations; private for-profit or not-for-profit agencies; private foundations, charities, or trusts; unions; or government agencies.

External Resources for Program Development

General resources include state grants, federal grants, foundations, endowments, business and industry payments for direct services, business and industry grants to education, and volunteer services. Chisman and Associates (1990, p. 247) call for greater funds at the federal, state, and local levels for teacher training and instructional technology and systems to promote greater coordination. State directors of adult education are a good source of current information on available funding.

State offices of adult education are responsible for the statewide administration of adult education by providing a system for application and approval of applications for funding, offering technical assistance, and monitoring and evaluating programs. They also have responsibility for regional adult education planning and interagency coordination with the multiple boards, departments, and services that fund adult education. State offices do so in an effort to improve services and eliminate duplication of services.

The adult education administrator needs to be familiar with funding sources and combination of funds to support a local program (Foster, 1990, p. 25). The administrator could investigate the resources by funding source (for example, Job Training Partnership Act or Federal Adult Education Act), category, or purpose (adult education and literacy, volunteer literacy, vocational skills, employment training and coordination, staff development, urban and ethnic education, bilingual education, library literacy, and so forth).

In order to seek external funding sources, one needs to understand the type of agency, its purpose, application process, deadlines, and typical grant (highest, lowest, and average amount). A funding agency, as reported by the Latino Institute in Chicago, may be variously called a fund, charitable trust, foundation, community trust, charity foundation, charities fund, or partnership program. Some examples are the Allstate Foundation, Kraft General Foods, Sara Lee Foundation, United Airlines Foundation, the Chicago Community Trust, *Chicago Sun-Times* Charity Foundation, and the *Chicago Tribune* Charities Fund. (See discussion of positive aspects of grant administration in Chapter Three and rationale for utilizing groups in Chapter Five.)

Gathering and utilizing input from external agencies is essential for the adult education administrator for program planning. Among the techniques that are used to gather information are surveys, focus groups, study groups, consensus groups, and town meetings.

Methods to Promote Program Development

Lewis and Dunlop (1991) report the results of a study ranking by frequency twenty-four factors associated with highly successful adult education programs. Six of the twenty-four factors cluster around administrative or managerial skills: effective administration and management philosophy, advertising and marketing, good facility or location, appropriate scheduling, pricing and budgeting, and customer support services.

Mason (1991, p. 7) cites "effective leadership with a positive vision of the potential of adult continuing education [as] the most important need" in the field. The vision is described as needing to be comprehensive, detailed, positive, inspiring, and linked to strategic planning. D. H. Smith (1989, p. 13) points out that "Adult and Continuing Education [ACE] and Human Resource Development [HRD] have more in common than they realize; each would benefit greatly if they would talk to one another." Among the recommendations are that ACE develop programs rather than courses and that ACE consider itself as a "consultant" to HRD and meet with both staffs for joint ventures.

In developing programs for institutions, agencies, or companies external to the adult education unit or parent organization, it is important to identify decision makers and cultivate their support (Mulcrone, 1990). Five types of decision makers are employee groups, labor unions, management, instructional providers, and others (advisory panels, committees, or task forces). These people are in a position to permit or encourage others to allocate program resources (liaison or coordination of staff, shared company and employee time for instruction, funds, facilities, materials, and so forth).

Decision makers also can influence other personnel to support programs. They may interact with internal decision makers from the adult education unit. Identifying decision makers is necessary before the roles and responsibilities of all associated can be clarified.

Another method to promote program development is to consider the entrepreneurial aspect. According to Smith and Offerman (1989), "Many ACE programs should be revenue-producing, profit-making entrepreneurial enterprises" and that any profit should be considered as a source for investment in future programs (p. 256). Amstutz (1992) calls the management of limited resources in higher education a new reality of "an entrepreneurial mode" (pp. 7–8). A key to institutional survival is outlined as the development of collaborative relationships from which institutions and other parties would mutually benefit. Examples include relationships with business (employee training and retraining), federal and state agencies (literacy hotline and national parks worker training), community agencies (literacy program), community colleges and universities (research and professional development), and other departments of the same institution (co-listing courses).

Accountability that demonstrates positive program outcomes promotes program growth. According to the Illinois Community College Board definition, accountability includes assessment requirements (as prescribed by accrediting bodies), productivity measures, student "right to know" requirements, college educational guarantees (verification of specific competencies related to programs of study), departmental program reviews, and strategic plans for college systems. (See the discussion of taxpayer scrutiny in Chapter Five and alternative accountability models in Chapter Nine.)

Successful Examples of Cooperative Ventures

What are some successful examples of cooperative ventures? Career cooperative programs generally pool the resources of secondary education, community colleges, and business and industry. Programs can include tech prep work readiness courses for high school seniors, job shadowing, applied sciences degree course work, business partnerships, work site experiences and employment, and internships.

Workplace Solutions is an employee assistance counseling program sponsored by a medical center, mental health center, high school and college school systems, and businesses to promote employee health. Attention is given to employee assistance with problems related to alcohol or drugs, emotional stress, marital or family relationships, finances, or other areas. A "What Do You Think of the Learning Resource Center?" survey probes level of quality of library services, needed changes, and services to add in the future.

Another successful example was the cooperation of adult education staff from William Rainey Harper College (Palatine, Illinois) and the personnel/ training staff of Motorola, Inc., to create the Integrative Workplace Basic Skills program. This program was designed for employees who had not made sufficient academic progress by other means of instruction. A full-time (forty-hour) program was jointly planned to include three components: classroom instruction followed by individual tutoring, group and individual counseling and team building, and application of learning from the first two components into production.

Learning community programs require coordination by administrators and/or faculty. The purpose of learning communities is to restructure the curriculum in ways that stress greater coherence among college courses and increased intellectual interaction among faculty and students. As described by the Washington Center for Improving the Quality of Undergraduate Education, some are coordinated studies, some team-taught linked classes, some cluster classes. Selected examples of these from the state of Washington are present at Edmonds Community College (coordinated studies—western civilization and study skills), Yakima Valley College (team-taught linked classes—biology and music appreciation), and Spokane Community College (cluster—American dreams and literature, English, and sociology). (See the discussion of learning organizations in Chapter Nine.)

An excellent use of student networks to help adult students overcome barriers associated with returning to school is cohort groups. For example, some fifty to sixty students at the Second Wind Program at Lakewood Community College, Minnesota, utilized these means: one-hour seminars held before classes, annotated phone directories, quarterly newsletters on off-campus news, support groups for common concerns, individual planning with counselors (who had also been returning adults), and the Adult Student Resource Center (National Institute for Staff and Organizational Development, pp. xiii–7).

An exemplary effort to strengthen existing Adult Basic Education programs in Massachusetts is SABES (System for Adult Basic Education Support). A comprehensive system, SABES serves programs funded by the state as well as those not funded to implement professional staff and program development and enhance communication. Ongoing adult education research and design is conducted through SABES, and the SABES office serves as a clearinghouse for publications of five decentralized support centers throughout the state. SABES connects teachers with educational theories, teaching techniques, materials, and public policy (Bureau of Adult Education, Massachusetts Department of Education, 1990–1991).

Future Issues Related to Resource Development

General issues that can act as deterrents to program growth are the lack of sufficient training for leaders such as department or division chairs (Filan, 1992), stereotypes about business and education, unwise approaches or reactions to financial problems (Kramer, 1989, p. 9; Amstutz, 1992, p. 7), lack of knowledge of institutional postures or attitudes toward programs (Kramer, 1989, pp. 10–11), lack of balance among responsibilities, lack of quality and credibility among programs (Miller, 1991, pp. 17–18), and lack of accountability (McKenna, 1991, p. 9).

What resource issues must be addressed to promote program growth and development? An issue for higher education is the need for flexible and responsive staff and structure in order to provide a greater portion of employee training (with estimates of up to $60 billion annually) than is currently provided by educational institutions to business and industry. Another issue involves the availability of proficient staff who can perform the great extent of job, task, and academic needs analyses that must be done in order to work with external agencies, companies, consortia, task forces, and cooperatives. (See the discussion of project need/problem statement in Chapter Three and staff development needs analysis in Chapter Six.)

A clearly defined policy and structure for educational guarantees is another resource issue. A program graduate could harm him- or herself on the job because of lack of competencies, and the school that provided the occupational training could be liable. Should a school guarantee the entire curriculum or specific programs only? Can human competencies really be viewed the same way as manufactured "products"? Will viewing adult and continuing education as a "product" with content and benefits help the administrator with marketing strategies?

Lack of a more flexible and equitable structure for service boundaries is another resource issue. Are community colleges bound to serve only those within its boundaries? What about free enterprise in services to business and industry outside proscribed school boundaries, especially if businesses took the initiative to request those services? Should universities be outside any district bounds, while community, technical, or junior colleges offer services only within a specified district?

Financial resources to permit public accommodation for persons with disabilities by existing private businesses that serve the public is a current issue. In addition to access at public universities and colleges, other places (theaters, museums, and private schools) where adult education services may be offered along with their primary purposes can be affected.

Several resource issues relate to staffing, especially in literacy programs. First, it is common knowledge that literacy programs are essentially staffed by part-time instructors who have little experience and training and leave the field within a few years. Another issue is having enough professional and support staff for comprehensive services for adult, family, and work force education and continued coordination with a number of public, community, volunteer, and business and industry service providers. The freestanding literacy center or program (Chisman and Associates, 1990, pp. 258–260), with its implications of being isolated from other social services and realistic training, parenting, or employment contexts, is another issue, as are appropriate assessment instruments and well-developed service delivery systems. Other challenges include staff expertise for design of local basic and applied research and demonstration projects in literacy, determination of effective means of recruitment and retention of disadvantaged adults, and documentation of effective means of educational gains of adult native and nonnative literacy (English as a second language) students. (See the discussion of literacy as a metaphor for adult education in Chapter Two and development of literacy instructors in Chapter Six.)

Finally, the adult and continuing education administrator must continue to deal in the future with many other resource issues: marginality or ambiguity, multiplicity or duplication of services (and thereby waste of resources), professionalism, record keeping for public or private accountability, accreditation, underprepared or unprepared students, increased technology, recruitment of multicultural faculty and staff, and student recruitment and retention strategies. (See the discussion of "at home" issues in Chapter Two and technology policy issues in Chapter Seven.)

References

Amstutz, D. "Managing Limited Resources: Entrepreneurs in Higher Education." *Adult Learning*, 1992, *3* (5), 7–9.

Bureau of Adult Education, Massachusetts Department of Education. *SABES: A Model State Literacy Resource Initiative, 1990–1991.* Boston: Bureau of Adult Education, Massachusetts Department of Education, 1990–1991.

Chisman, F. P., and Associates. *Leadership for Literacy.* San Francisco: Jossey-Bass, 1990.

Dahl, D. A. "Resources." In A. B. Knox and Associates, *Developing, Administering, and Evaluating Adult Education.* San Francisco: Jossey-Bass, 1986.

Filan, G. L. "The Trick to Being a Community College Chair." *Leadership Abstracts,* 1992, *5* (1).

Foster, S. E. "Upgrading the Skills of Literacy Professionals." In F. P. Chisman and Associates, *Leadership for Literacy.* San Francisco: Jossey-Bass, 1990.

Knox, A. B. "Educational Leadership and Program Administration." In J. M. Peters, P. Jarvis, and Associates, *Adult Education: Evolution and Achievements in a Developing Field of Study.* San Francisco: Jossey-Bass, 1991.

Kramer, J. L. "Continuing Education and the New Fiscal Strategies." *Continuing Higher Education,* 1989, *37* (3), 9–13.

Lewis, C. H., and Dunlop, C. C. "Successful and Unsuccessful Adult Education Programs: Perceptions, Explanations, and Implications." In T. J. Sork (ed.), *Mistakes Made and Lessons Learned: Overcoming Obstacles to Successful Programming.* New Directions for Adult and Continuing Education, no. 49. San Francisco: Jossey-Bass, 1991.

McKenna, B. "The Trials of Accreditation." *On Campus,* 1991, *11* (2), 8–9, 11.

Mason, R. C. "Positive, Visionary Leadership: An Organization's Most Successful Component." *Adult Learning,* 1991, *3* (3), 7, 13.

Miller, D. A. "No Classes, No Campus, No Problem: Non-Traditional Degree-Granting Programs." *Adult Learning,* 1991, *3* (3), 17–19.

Mulcrone, P. "An Inquiry into Instructional and Administrative Practices: A Collaborative Cycles Model." Unpublished doctoral dissertation, Northern Illinois University, De Kalb, 1990.

National Institute for Staff and Organizational Development, Community College Leadership Program, University of Texas at Austin. "Adult Student Development in an Off-Campus Setting." *Innovation Abstracts,* 1991, *13* (7).

Smith, D. H. "Adult and Continuing Education and Human Resource Development—Present Competitors, Potential Partners." *Lifelong Learning: An Omnibus of Practice and Research,* 1989, *12* (7), 13–17.

Smith, D. H., and Offerman, M. J. "The Management of Adult and Continuing Education." In S. B. Merriam and P. M. Cunningham (eds.), *Handbook of Adult and Continuing Education.* San Francisco: Jossey-Bass, 1989.

PATRICIA MULCRONE *is professor and chair of the Adult Educational Development Department at William Rainey Harper College, Palatine, Illinois.*

A historic reflection on the role of adult education in focusing on issues as a prelude to informed, democratic decision making is juxtaposed to a more dominant instrumental and corporate view of the field.

Identifying and Dealing with Educational, Social, and Political Issues

Thomas W. Heaney

In his now classic text, *The Meaning of Adult Education,* Eduard Lindeman admonished the fledgling field that adult education could become an agency of progress only "if its short-term goal of self-improvement can be made compatible with a longtime, experimental but resolute policy of changing the social order" (Lindeman, 1989, p. 105). This chapter is about what adult education almost was and still could be. The medium is the message, since to reflect on the history of our field is already to identify and navigate educational, social, and political issues that lie at the core of our self-understanding and our practice as administrators of adult education.

Founding Vision: Building a Democratic Society

The importance of adult learning to the empowerment of society is never so clear as in the formative years of a democracy. Our earliest identification of the adult education enterprise in the United States was embraced, as in the writings of Lindeman and others, within a broader quest for freedom and participation in decisions that affect day-to-day life. To cast off restraints, to decide resolutely and wisely the course of our affairs, we must identify and comprehend the social and political issues of our day. This is an educational task of monumental consequence, and on it rests the success or failure of our most basic freedoms.

Forums for Reflection and Action. Adult education was, first, a forum for reflection and action, the lyceum and the town hall meeting being two sides of the same coin, one emphasizing mutual self-education, the other strategy building and decision making (Bode, 1956). During the early part of this century, over three hundred workers' schools awakened among the U.S. working class first a questioning, then disquiet and resistance, and eventually a historic labor movement (Hellyer and Schulman, 1990). Understanding of embedded contradictions in the social fabric grew in the expanded consciousness of liberal studies.

The democratic function of adult education is nowhere as evident as in the ongoing work of the Highlander Center in Tennessee. Beginning in the 1930s with the education of workers in the newly formed unions of the South and continuing into the civil rights era with the education of that movement's leaders, Highlander Center has consistently nurtured a vision of political and economic democracy through reflection and action. For Myles Horton, Highlander's founder, who believed that "people have within themselves the potential, intelligence, courage and ability to solve their own problems," adult education always began with "a goal arising out of a social problem that the students perceive" (Horton, 1990, p. 153).

The historic identification of adult education with democratic social change is evident in numerous social and revolutionary movements, from the Southwide Citizenship Schools in the early 1950s to more recent campaigns for literacy that have accompanied a transition from dictatorship to democracy. As demonstrated in the work of Paulo Freire, people first learn to retell their history, then make history through reconstructive action (Freire, 1970).

Gaining a Voice in Shaping the Future. Literacy in the work of Freire and others becomes a metaphor for adult education. Adult education is the task of learning to name our world, coming to understand the connections between seemingly disparate elements of our experience, naming our reality in order to control it. In a word, literacy is about the identification of issues. It is a mastery not only of language but of the reality that language communicates. Literacy is not the acquisition of words but the acquisition of a voice in matters that affect day-to-day life. Hence, both literacy and adult education in this view are about liberation. They are about dialogue, about shared understandings, about empowerment for collective political and economic action. (See the discussion of literacy issues in Chapter One and the development of literacy instructors in Chapter Six.)

The content and not the process of literacy is the key to these claims for a liberatory adult pedagogy. Vital, experienced-based texts are far more important than pedagogical methods in achieving literacy. Adults learn to read and write their world before the relevance of books and print are self-evident. Adult education is not merely coming to know new facts; it is coming to know what we know, reflecting on our experience, so that knowledge becomes a power in us—a power to take action in a rational and decisive manner. Adult education can, like the reading of texts, provoke reflection and critical judgment as a prelude to change. Adult education is learning to swim in a sea of issues that otherwise threatens to drown us. This is the insight with which Lindeman, Meiklejohn, and other visionary educators launched the adult education movement in the United States.

Professionalization and the Waning of Social Purpose

Unfortunately, the origins of our field are not so simple. There was a competing vision that gained ascendancy by the 1970s. Opening the doors to immigrants from Europe at the turn of the century represented not only an opportunity for a country in need of skilled workers but, in the view of many, a clear danger as well. Those fearful of the dilution of the United States' uniqueness saw in adult education a prized tool for the homogenization of those immigrants and a purging of foreign influence. From the government-sponsored Americanization program to the more liberal work of Jane Addams and the settlement house movement, the goal shifted from empowerment to adaptation, from decision making to conformity. The task was no longer to create democracy but to buttress and support a social order that proclaimed democratic values, while ritualizing the practice of democracy in once-a-year, partisan elections.

The Cult of Efficiency. Industrialization, the growth of the military in two world wars, and the expansion of government bureaucracy demanded a new role for adult education. Americans needed the knowledge and skills to operate competitively and efficiently the machinery of state. Critical reflection on issues and time-consuming participation in decision making were not only inefficient but potentially divisive. Workers' education began to focus on procedures and operations rather than on analysis of economic relations within the workplace. The former would yield a more productive work force; the latter would breed discontent. Even unions came to insist that the educational needs of their rank and file were better served by training than by encouraging reflection on issues that might lead workers to a critique of an entrenched union bureaucracy. In this new economy of adult learning, content was no longer at issue. The content was reduced to the social or workplace environment to which the adult learner was to be adapted. Emphasis shifted from content to method in defining the practice of adult education.

Two related developments supported this shift in focus from substance to method—from democracy to efficiency—in adult education practice. The first was the redefinition of adult educators as high technicians, transforming practitioners of the art of adult learning into technicians of the science of andragogy. As the fledgling field developed its how-to manuals and systems for the administration of an adult education enterprise, questions of social or political purpose such as those raised by Lindeman and Horton receded into the background. Identifying and dealing with social and political issues became problematic for self-proclaimed neutral service providers who facilitated the acquisition of appropriate knowledge and skills in response to needs prescribed by employers or by governmental guardians. The second development was the redefinition of adult education as a profession, promoted by the expansion of schooling into adulthood and the formalization of adult education in credit-granting institutions that provided a stable and respectable base for an upwardly mobile, aspiring professional class of adult education practitioners.

The "Clientization" of Everyone. Expanding markets for educational services provided the rationale for turning lifelong learning into lifelong schooling. Adults "needed" professional assistance not only in the task of learning but also in identifying appropriate learning projects. As learners became clients of trainers and other educational providers, it was an easy transition from marketing services for reluctant learners to mandatory continuing education, all in the name of efficiency. Research on why adults participated or, more frequently, failed to participate in adult education had failed to identify a cure for the deficiencies of dropouts and other resisters. Henceforth, in many instances adult educators achieved forced annual diagnosis and rehabilitation of their clients, but without accountability.

Social Control and the Disappearance of Issues. In his analysis of power Steven Lukes (1974) observes that the most effective and far-reaching exercise of power does not rest on the use of overt force that is expensive, inefficient, and likely to engender counterforce. The most effective power is exercised by the control of knowledge. What we understand of our history, what we believe to be realistic expectations for ourselves and our families, our understanding of concepts such as race, gender, or class—concepts by which we lay hold of our experience and evaluate day-to-day life—these can enslave us or set us free. Therein lies the power of the educator. Two visions of how that power is to be used have shaped adult education in the United States: one a vision of adult education as a means of deepening our understanding of contemporary issues so we can become full and able participants in deciding the direction of social and political history, the other a vision of adult education as a means of implementing a future that the learner neither understands nor helps to create.

Redefining a Corporate Model for Education

It is inevitable, perhaps, that we adopt the practices and language of our benefactors. The adult education enterprise in the United States, that almost-movement of the 1920s and 1930s, now resembles the corporations it has served so efficiently for half a century. Its bottom-line thinking and preoccupation with market share have benefited no one so much as adult education practitioners. While it has rewarded the most diligent and persevering learners with a competitive edge in jobs and social status, it has manufactured needs even more quickly than services in emulation of industry's marketers. Encouraged by expanded investment in human capital, adult educators now produce consumers of education as their flagship product line.

Central to a corporate model of adult education is administration, and administration requires control. It is essentially a hierarchical function even if performed collectively by two or more individuals. As a result, the goals and objectives of adult education organizations are seldom determined or even shaped by learners. In this sense, administration is generally inimical to participation and democracy. Learners are not expected to be informed on matters of policy, even when that policy affects their own learning. Except for those instances in which institutional interests prevail, as when public subsidies for adult education are required, the inclusion of social and political issues or other policy-related matters within the curriculum is deemed inappropriate and threatens the assumed neutrality of the educational enterprise. On the other hand, adult education activities organized for the purposes of democratic social action avoid the corporate model and its administrative function. (See the discussion of foundations and corporations in Chapter Three.)

Administration as the Juggler's Act. Despite the functional limitations of the corporate model of education (and because of the older tradition of adult education grounded in the building of democracy), many adult educators strain against their corporate traces and have sought ways to focus their art on more liberatory aims. They have sought to be critically reflective in their work as well as to facilitate critical reflection in the learners whom they serve. In seeking to restore social purpose to their work, they have identified at least two common strategies for redefining the corporate model for adult education.

Critical Analysis of "At Home" Issues. An honest and forthright analysis of the social functions and consequences of our own adult education practice is a place to begin. Adult educators who unquestioningly believe their own advertising copy are unlikely to aid learners who struggle to understand the issues embedded in their day-to-day lives. The most important educational, social, and political issues to comprehend are generally those that implicate us, because they are the issues about which we can take action. Administrators can facilitate a process of reform that involves circles of staff and learners engaged in the critical evaluation of program and the identification of barriers to improvement—including institutional barriers. This participatory task is adult education in its most progressive sense: adults engaged in the task of understanding their reality in order to change it. (See the discussion of resource issues in Chapter One and technology policy issues in Chapter Seven.)

Navigating Bureaucratic Limits and Discovering Open Spaces. Analysis of our practice will undoubtedly disclose that bureaucracies thrive on the illusion of impenetrability and changelessness. It is this illusion—the internalized axiom that things will be as they are—that prevents action and thwarts change. On the other hand, all bureaucratic systems are loosely woven fabrics with room for those who study their scope and contours to take initiatives and create pockets of resistance. Contradictions embedded in the educational milieu, such as the principle of academic freedom, make it possible for sensitive and socially conscious educators to link issues of race, gender, and class with the prescribed curriculum. Administrators, building on adult education's commitment to lifelong learning, can facilitate this expansion of the curriculum through the ongoing staff development of teachers. Such development activities could include workshops critically analyzing gender or class stereotypes in the curriculum, the relationship between race and employment, or reflection on and application of current legislation on access or sexual harassment.

Models with "Wiggle Room" for Action

In combination with these strategies, several models for socially responsible, issue-oriented adult education—two generated within the corporate sector itself—have evolved over the past decade.

TQM and Freire's Circulo de Cultura. Total quality management (TQM), highly regarded as an administrative model for maximizing productivity in the workplace, emphasizes collective responsibility, decentralized controls, and participatory decision making (Wellins, Byham, and Wilson, 1991). At least on the surface, it embodies features that characterized Freire's approach to organizing adult literacy education in Brazil, Chile, Guinea-Bissau, and other developing countries. In both TQM and Freire's work, a circle of learner-workers begins with an analysis of their collective experience in order to understand it. Building on that understanding, they make decisions affecting future action. TQM, of course, operates within the narrow and administratively defined context of the worker. That is, while a circle of workers is empowered to identify and solve problems at their work site and then implement the solution, the workers are generally unable to impose remedies on administrative problems, even when those problems directly affect them (Nemoto, 1987).

Freire's circulo de cultura also operates within prescribed limits, however. Solutions to all problems are not within the grasp of a study circle, even in a revolution. Here, as in the corporate world, the most important issues to comprehend are generally those that implicate us because they are the issues about which we can take action. Even in an idealized democratic context we cannot prescribe the actions of others except as they affect the fundamental rights and obligations of all.

TQM is an effective tool for legitimizing the introduction of issues into the otherwise instrumental content of peer education in the workplace. The development of quality circles is already an educational function, with participants themselves being peer resources to one another in problem posing—a necessary first step in the task of problem solving. Furthermore, quality circles foster democracy at the work site to the extent that participants retain the power to make decisions and act (Semler, 1989).

Strategic Planning as Participatory Research. Strategic planning, to the extent that it involves all those concerned with its outcomes in an ongoing cycle of reflection and action, also fosters the identification of issues in a democratic context. While more formally structured, it is similar in its underlying assumptions to participatory research, which affirms the importance in problem solving of having those whose problem it is be part of the solution. In a sequence of steps, participants in strategic planning review the stated mission; identify strengths, weaknesses, and strategies for change; establish priorities; and take action (Rice, 1990). The planning cycle of reflection and action is repeated regularly. While the process is limited by parameters set within the corporate mission, critical reflection even on the mission itself is possible. (See the discussion of active learner participation in staff development in Chapter Six and learning contracts in Chapter Nine.)

Both TQM and strategic planning are built on the realization that adults are more committed to implementing solutions that they have helped to create and, therefore, more likely to be productive. While both mechanisms can be used to exploit workers, the "open spaces" within them make possible the identification of issues and open the door to democratically determined resolution of contradictions.

Partnerships with the Movers Within Movements. The most far-reaching strategy for redefining the corporate model is found in partnerships between business and social change organizations and groups. Business and industry have occasionally worked hand in hand with local reform organizations to their mutual benefit. For example, national attention has been focused on leading corporations in Chicago that have formed partnerships with local school councils in connection with that city's school reform movement. In other areas of the country, businesses have joined forces with economic development corporations and with neighborhood self-help organizations. Such alliances broaden the context for the identification of issues beyond those narrowly defined within the workplace and encompass the impact of the workplace itself on the community and on society. (See the discussion of external resources in Chapter One, adequate resources in Chapter Three, and corporate resources in Chapter Nine.)

Similar examples are found among educational institutions that make their resources available to community-based and democratically controlled organizations, many of which are committed to social, political, and economic change. Examples include the Center for Urban Affairs at Northwestern University and the Center for Community Education and Action with its linkages to the University of Massachusetts. Such institutions are, on occasion, able to transcend the barrier of their proclaimed neutrality by supporting social and political citizen action with critical analysis, knowledge, and skills.

Choosing a Path for the Future. The identification of issues is not a minor task for adult educators. It is, at least in the origins of the U.S. tradition of the field, the central preoccupation of adult learners as they seek a voice in those matters that directly affect their lives. Whether in the workplace or at home, the democratic ideal of collective problem posing, strategy building, and action requires a critically informed public, cognizant of issues and confident in its power to act. Adult education has evolved in two paths. One has facilitated democratic reflection and action through a critical identification of issues; the other has served to domesticate learners, ignore contradictions, and adjust minds to the inevitable conformities of a mass society. In the older tradition, adult educators exercised leadership and vision: leadership by building democratic leadership, and vision by not merely seeing what is but foreseeing what could be.

References

Bode, C. *The American Lyceum*. New York: Oxford University Press, 1956.

Freire, P. *Pedagogy of the Oppressed*. New York: Seabury, 1970.

Hellyer, M. R., and Schulman, B. "Workers' Education." In S. B. Merriam and P. M. Cunningham (eds.), *Handbook of Adult and Continuing Education*. San Francisco: Jossey-Bass, 1989.

Horton, M. *The Long Haul*. New York: Doubleday, 1990.

Lindeman, E. *The Meaning of Adult Education*. Norman: Oklahoma Research Center for Continuing Professional and Higher Education, 1989.

Lukes, S. *Power: A Radical View*. London: Macmillan, 1974.

Nemoto, M. *Total Quality Control for Management*. Englewood Cliffs, N.J.: Prentice Hall, 1987.

Rice, C. S. *Strategic Planning for the Small Business*. Holbrook, Mass.: Bob Adams, 1990.

Semler, R. "Managing Without Managers." *Harvard Business Review,* Sept.–Oct. 1989, pp. 76–84.

Wellins, R. S., Byham, W. E., and Wilson, J. M. *Empowered Teams: Creating Self-Directed Work Groups That Improve Quality, Productivity, and Participation*. San Francisco: Jossey-Bass, 1991.

THOMAS W. HEANEY is a member of the graduate faculty of adult continuing education at Northern Illinois University and director of the Lindeman Center for Community Empowerment through Education in Chicago.

The art and science of grants management is an acquired skill for the grant seeker who comes to understand the types of grants, the grant guidelines and resources, and the four major stages of grant writing and administration.

Managing Multiple Funding Sources and Writing Grant Documents

Ernest W. Brewer

To date, little has been written that is specifically designed to help educators who work with adults learn how to manage multiple funding sources and how to write grant documents that will secure external funds. Typically, available literature tells how to deal with adolescent programs and institutional bureaucracies or how to find external financing to fund such programs, but little else. Most external grant programs for education service the nation's youth programs. For this reason, most existing information and networking efforts relate to known procedures and methodologies on how to secure and operate successful adolescent programs. However, more adult education programs are appearing (such as the Educational Opportunity Center, Veterans Upward Bound, Migrant's High School Equivalency Program, various literacy programs, job retraining, and so forth), which has created the need for an overview and guidelines for the changing roles, responsibilities, and strategies for adult education program administrators.

New grant seekers concentrate on getting funds for their potential projects. To obtain such funds, they must master the art and science of writing effective grant proposals. Grant writers must be particularly skillful in the overall scope of grant writing, especially in this era of increased competition for grants (Bailey, 1990). Hall (1988) shares this view, stating that there is still "fierce competition among an increasing number of applicants. . . . It is even more important that one know how to prepare an effective proposal" (p. 19). Because educators who work with adults lack the kind of resources available to other groups of grant seekers, this chapter seeks to describe the necessary components of a successful grant proposal for an adult education program. In addition, this chapter outlines steps the grant administrator needs to take after the process of grant solicitation is completed and the grant monies are received. At this point, the task remains of managing the project (or multiple projects) to achieve maximum results.

Although program management may seem relatively simple at first glance, it involves a number of considerations and guidelines with respect to staffing, program logistics, equipment, documentation, auditing, instrument development, recruitment, and compliance with many complex internal and external grant requirements. The grants administrator must be able to fulfill these and other management obligations in order to receive future funding consideration. Successful administration of funded projects by adult education professionals helps increase the grant administrators' abilities, knowledge, experience, contacts, and visibility, which in turn help in securing future grants. A direct correlation exists between effectively managing funded projects and receiving future grants. This is especially true because of the exponential growth of worthy programs seeking external funds. In a period of decreased resources and reduced awards, more and more grant makers are requiring clear evidence of strong institutional management (Bailey, 1990; Lefferts, 1990; Brewer, Achilles, and Fuhriman, 1993).

Things to Consider Before Writing a Proposal

Before committing time and energy to writing a proposal, the grant seeker must be prepared to consider what is really involved in the effective administration of grants. Assuring compliance with various rules and regulations involves the many "strings" or special requirements that may come with the grant. These strings may control, at least in part, how the program is run. For example, a federal grant may affect staffing decisions, client recruitment, and measurement instruments. At least part of the funding resources must be directed toward documentation. Is the target population meeting the program goals? How can change be measured? What tracking system is available to measure short- and long-term project effectiveness? Because external grant monies must be accounted for in detail, an effective disbursal and auditing system must be in place.

As stated earlier, grants management is not merely the process of obtaining a grant. It also includes hiring and training support staff, identifying and recruiting adult clients, implementing program goals and objectives in a timely manner, enacting the promised execution of program operations, and establishing instruments for program evaluation. While it is highly gratifying to secure external funds, prospective administrators need to know beforehand that this is only the beginning of a simultaneously exciting, frustrating, fulfilling, nerve-wracking, exhilarating venture. The implementation and maintenance stages may seem like a roller coaster because of the many ups and downs the administrator will experience throughout the project period. Unannounced audits and site visitations, monthly or even weekly progress reports, payroll expenditures, and contact with the program's target population add to the tension, especially if staffing is part-time, temporary, and contingent on future grant funding. Tension can also be caused by adult clients served by the program moving away, dropping out, or even suddenly increasing in number.

Retaining support staff can pose particular problems if their employment relates directly to the potential for future grant funding. Without the security of some employment continuity, staff may leave for other, more permanent positions within the administrator's organization but outside the grant program or outside the institution. This turnover may require frequent recruiting and training of new support staff, which in turn can affect program continuity, both for the adult clients serviced by the program and for the internal monitoring aspects of the program.

On the positive side is the recognition that the program serves a direct public good, a point that some local communities and municipalities formally acknowledge or that adult clients demonstrate during and following program participation. On the negative side, however, are the headaches of meeting project deadlines, recruiting staff and clients, and dealing with the unforeseen demands of the host institution and those imposed by the external grant source for information.

Successful grantees often touch on the positive aspect of writing and managing multiple grants, but there are obviously many potential negatives, seldom mentioned, that a potential grant writer should consider before writing a proposal. The grant writer should try to mitigate these negatives prior to seeking external funds.

It is also essential that the grant seeker assess his or her capability to respond to grant opportunities. Hall (1988) poses two questions: "Have you assessed the competence of your institution?" and "Does your organization have the essential support systems?" (p. 16). Answers to these questions will dictate whether one should proceed to the next stage and whether one is eligible to respond to certain requests for proposals (RFPs) or requests for applications (RFAs) that may be of interest to the institution. If the answers to these questions are affirmative, one then needs to assess how competitive one will be in responding to a specific RFP or RFA. Is one eligible to respond? How competitive is the grant? That is, will the funding agency award only one grant, or will thirty or more different grant awards be made? How much lead time is needed to work on the proposal or application and meet the deadline?

Brewer, Achilles, and Fuhriman (1993) list items to consider from personal and institutional viewpoints before one begins to develop a proposal. Following are some questions from the personal point of view: "Do I have enough time to write the proposal and submit it by the deadline date? Can I maintain my current job responsibilities while developing a grant proposal? Am I willing to put a high level of energy into the proposal to ensure that it is competitive and not just mediocre?" (p. 28). The answers to these questions, along with the following questions about institutional commitment, will help one decide if one should proceed in responding to a grant application: "Is this grant activity within the mission and scope of my institution or agency? Does my institution have the necessary facilities and resources to conduct the activities of the project? If so, will my institution commit the needed facilities and resources? If matching funds are required, can or will my institution be able to meet these requirements? If the funds are cut off and the program is dropped, what effect will it have on my institution?" (p. 28). Adult education administrators who begin to write proposals without examining these issues often end up not completing the proposal, not meeting the deadline, or, if funded, not being able to implement the project and meet the requirements of the grant.

Positive Aspects of Grant Administration. Perhaps the most obvious positive aspect of being awarded a grant is gaining new resources to help meet an important need within the organization or community. A grant provides the funding to set up a program independent of the organization's usual hierarchical constraints. Although the grant writer is obviously part of the organization, he or she is not solely dependent on it for funds to operate the program. The grant administrator of multiple grants doubtless will have some release time, additional support personnel, and autonomy to set his or her own work routine, expand options for professional travel, and meet professionals related to the project focus. Project funds may support new equipment, educational materials, graduate assistantships, release time of other faculty, or other resources. (See the discussion of external resources for program development in Chapter One and rationale for utilizing groups in Chapter Five.)

Another positive aspect is that one can typically use the work done on a funded project to provide material for a professional presentation or published paper. The administrator will be affecting the lives of adult clients who turn to the program for assistance and adding to the knowledge base of adult education. In effect, one can learn from the experiences of clients, staff, and one's own administrative actions to help others set up similar programs that can, in turn, affect larger numbers of adult clients nationwide. Finally, if it can be demonstrated that the project or projects are well run and successful and that they contribute positively to the organization, the administrator will gain personal and professional recognition.

Negative Aspects of Grant Administration. First, one needs to beware of red tape, red tape, and more red tape! Because of the managerial, fiduciary, and legal responsibilities involved, one must be prepared to document continually. Paperwork may seem overwhelming at times, but it represents documentation of what the program does and how it functions. It presents to the grantor, the institution, and other interested organizations one's accomplishments in fulfilling the requirements of the grant. Monthly or even weekly reports will typically entail the construction of complex tracking systems based on program goals and actual outcomes. Every detail of client correspondence, including letters, notes, conversations, and telephone calls, must be included in the reports. Individual client files of accepted and rejected applicants may include an application form, various evaluation instruments, client activity responses, and rationale statements that justify staff decisions and activities. The problems of maintaining a temporary support staff can make documentation especially difficult, depending on how well the staff maintains client records.

In addition, the grants administrator will be held accountable to two masters: the organization and the grant funding agency. One's institution will invariably require that the administrator carry out responsibilities associated with one's position. This may include teaching classes, overseeing students, serving on a variety of committees, directing thesis research, or conducting relevant research for the institution itself. Sometimes a conflict of interest, such as project-related travel, may take one away from other duties.

Not everyone in the organization will be as enthusiastic about the project as the grants administrator, and he or she may not receive the organizational support initially felt when securing the grant. For example, one could face jealousy from peers who may resent the attention, prestige, or autonomy the program garners. Others may resent the competition for classroom space or even for parking space that the program creates. Regardless of funding, an adult education program will consume some resources of the institution, and one's peers may not always be understanding of such an altruistic program.

Another downside to grant administration is the need to always be prepared for, or subjected to, site visits and audits and a corresponding high level of accountability. Expectations from the funding agency can run extremely high, so one can expect to learn to deal with pressure. Typically, one can expect any external grant program to require detailed monthly or even weekly reports on the targeted adult population. Academic progress reports, travel expenditures, and other costs must be meticulously noted and reported. Of course, monthly reports eventually lead to a larger annual report that provides a more comprehensive overview and evaluation of the program. The amount of paperwork involved in this report can be overwhelming.

Another potential negative aspect of grant administration involves status within the organization. Unless the grant or grants are very large, one may find the project relegated to a subordinate role in which the project is assigned second-rate space, furnishings, equipment, and supplies. In this position, the program may be subjected to several relocations to meet the organization's varying needs, to the loss of access to equipment, or to recurring scheduling difficulties with respect to space.

Last, continuation of funding always creates problems for the administrator, along with the stress of dealing with time lines and meeting deadlines. Unless the program can generate autonomous funding, one faces the prospect of applying and reapplying for funds to sustain the program. Reapplication naturally entails competing for ever-scarcer dollars and possibly losing the program should it not be re-funded.

Different Hats Worn by a Grants Administrator. A grants administrator must possess numerous talents, including the polish of a politician, the dexterity of a juggler, the communication skills of a public relations specialist, the tact of a diplomat, and the organizational skills of a master manager. In other words, effective administrators tend to be generalists (Ross, 1990). Following are some major roles necessary for managing multiple grants: administrator, public relations person, marketer, researcher, negotiator, fiscal officer, entrepreneur, strategist, evaluator, planner, innovator, persuader, devil's advocate, interpreter, personnel manager, and visionary (Brewer, Achilles, and Fuhriman, 1993).

Reif-Lehrer (1989) states that the way in which one writes the grant proposals tells the readers a lot about the potential grants administrator. She lists the following questions that may be associated with the hats one wears in administering grants: "Do you show originality of thought? Do you plan ahead—and do so with ingenuity? Do you have good managerial skills? How do you handle a budget? How meticulous are you?" (p. 82). A person's administrative talent and execution of skills will determine how he or she performs as an administrator and, ultimately, whether the project will be re-funded.

Wearing many hats is necessary for the administrator to deal with and direct the diversity of people and situations of a grant program. In addition to working with support staff, colleagues, and administrators within one's own organization, one must deal with the general public, potential adult clients, grantee auditors and on-site inspectors, and interested peers and visitors to the program. Situational crises will test one's temperament and resolve: support staff who precipitously leave the program or inflict their incompetence on one's efforts; disgruntled clients; payroll problems; program inquiries; travel; on-site visitations; measurement instrument designs; and weekly, monthly, or annual reports.

Types of Grants

It is imperative that one identify some key characteristics of a potential project for which one is interested in writing a proposal. Hall (1988) stresses that most sources of funding limit their grant awards through at least one of the following four considerations: "What is the function [research, development, service, training, or demonstration] of the project you are proposing?"; "In what field [adult education, technology, and so on] is your project?"; "Who [unemployed, displaced workers, illiterates, and so on] will benefit from your project?"; and "What are the geographic parameters [regional, local, and so on] of your project?"

Regarding function, one must first ensure that the project does more than merely report on or describe some sort of phenomenon. For example, instead of soliciting grant monies to identify a problem, one should focus on the benefits of the project. One will be more likely to succeed if the project involves helping a target population by developing a program or methodology to service an identifiable need. Second, one must clearly identify the field in which one plans to conduct the program. Third, one should clearly identify the target adult population, perhaps with a profile or description. Finally, one should describe the geographic boundaries of the program in terms of the area (a county, a region of the state, or even several states) from which the targeted adult clients would be drawn.

Grant sources frequently spell out the parameters for which a proposal may qualify. By answering the previously listed questions, one will be able to determine whether the project under consideration relates to a purpose outlined by the funding source (usually a public source of funds) or whether the idea originates with the grant writer. The grant proposal may therefore be either solicited or unsolicited.

Solicited Grants. Funding for solicited grants typically comes from the local, state, or federal government. Solicited proposals are prepared in response to a formal written request by a funding agency. In other words, there is competition for the grants, and they are not earmarked for any particular person or group. They are won via a grant writer's skills, creativity, and the merits of the proposal. Such grants may set forth broad guidelines within which a grant writer may operate. Typically, solicited projects are initiated by an RFP if it is for a contract or an RFA if it is for a grant. Some examples of federal solicited grants are the School Dropout Demonstration Program, Migrant Education High School Equivalency Program, and the Demonstration Centers for the Retaining of Dislocated Workers program. One must closely examine any proposal in response to an RFP or RFA to ensure that one is adhering to all of the funding agency's guidelines (Hall, 1988). This type of grant has a definite submission deadline that is given in the application package. The package usually includes a set of criteria for the evaluation of the proposal. The overall proposal length for solicited grants is, typically, significantly longer (twenty to eighty pages) than that of an unsolicited grant.

Unsolicited Grants. These grants are typically supported by the private sector, the primary sources of funding being philanthropic foundations (Brewer, Achilles, and Fuhriman, 1993). Unsolicited proposals are more difficult to get funded because of the number of grant funders that limit awards to specific priorities. Such grants typically are awarded to provide general support, project grants, fellowships, and scholarships. Bowker and Associates (1992) suggest that no other area of philanthropy is as "misunderstood and misused as that of private foundations[;] ... as many as 80 percent of all applications to private foundations are inappropriate or misdirected" (p. ix).

Lefferts (1990) states that the majority of all proposals submitted are unsolicited. He notes that there is "more latitude in the form and content of unsolicited proposals" (p. 10). The requirements of foundations and corporations are seldom as stringent as those of RFPs and RFAs. Hall (1988) notes that unsolicited proposals need to do a better job of "convincing the funding source of the merit of the idea, the need for the program, and the capability of the submitting agency to administer a successful project" (p. 9).

Four Major Stages of Grant Writing and Administration

Adult educators who may have an interest in securing external funds to support and manage multiple projects need to remain cognizant of the following areas: exploring grants, writing multiple grants, managing grants, and closing out grants. Each of these areas is significant for the adult education administrator interested in developing comprehensive programs.

Stage 1: Exploring Grants. To become an effective proposal writer for multiple grants dealing with education for adults, one's first step should involve becoming familiar with the various U.S. Department of Education programs, their general purposes and requirements, and their deadline dates (Brewer, Achilles, and Fuhriman, 1993). One must become familiar with various funding sources, the individuals who provide information about solicited education programs, and federal government appropriations and allocations. Funding agencies range from federal sources and private foundations to corporations (Solomon, 1991; Brewer, Achilles, and Fuhriman, 1993). One must know where to look for information about funding, such as in libraries, offices of sponsored research, newspapers, and so on (Stopka and Beland, 1989).

Foundations and Corporations. A good place to begin looking for grants from foundations is *The Foundation Directory.* More in line with the adult education administrator's interest, *The National Guide to Funding in Higher Education* source book is intended as a starting point for grant seekers looking for funding support for education. This guide contains information on more than three thousand grant funding foundations that have shown a substantial interest in programs in education. Those two major publications are produced by the Foundation Center. The Taft Corporation publishes a two-volume set of reference directories that combine information on corporate and foundation funding sources—*The Directory of Corporate and Foundation Givers* and *The Foundation Reporter* (Sparks, 1989; Stopka and Beland, 1989; Solomon, 1991). These sources are very important when searching for opportunities for unsolicited proposals. (See the discussion of corporate models in Chapter Two.)

Federal Register (FR) and Code of Federal Regulations (CFR). The FR and the CFR are the official federal government documents that inform the public and, more specifically, the educator working with adults, of the various federal grant programs. Documents published in the daily FR keep the annual CFR current. These documents make changes to the appropriate CFR volume.

The FR is published every weekday, except on legal holidays, by the Office of the Federal Register. It is available at all depository libraries and is distributed through the superintendent of documents. Having access to this daily publication is paramount in monitoring the federal rules and regulations, proposed rules, and notices about potential RFAs because it provides the latest information regarding applications, grant requirements, and grant regulations.

Published annually, the CFR is a basic component of the Federal Register publication system. It is a codification of the regulations of the various federal agencies and is divided into fifty titles according to subject matter. Each title represents a broad area that is subject to federal regulation. As an educator who works with adults, one will doubtless be particularly interested in Title 34, which deals with education, and probably Title 29, which deals with labor.

Catalog of Federal Domestic Assistance (CFDA). This publication may be the single most valuable reference for information about federal funding. Published annually in June with an update in December, it is designed to assist users in identifying programs that meet specific objectives. The *CFDA* includes a number of indexes to help users locate specific programs of interest, determine eligibility, and obtain information on application deadlines for programs. It contains both general information and specific details, such as names and phone numbers for program project officers. For example, for an educator interested in seeking grant support for adults, the following programs may be of interest: Adult Education—National Discretionary Programs, CFDA 84.191; National Workplace Literacy Program, CFDA 84.198; Adult Education for the Homeless, CFDA 84.192; and the High School Equivalency Program, CFDA 84.141. Many public and university libraries carry the *CFDA*, as do the national, state, and local offices of federal departments and agencies. It can be purchased from the same office that distributes the *FR* and the *CFR* (Gelatt, 1989).

Guide to Funding in Education. This annual provides an accurate, detailed description of the federal programs offering financial assistance to local and state educational agencies (LEAs and SEAs), postsecondary institutions, and other public and private organizations and agencies working in the field of education. For each program, the *Guide* provides a program purpose, quick check, key facts, any program restrictions, the grant funding process, award information, and the person to contact for more information.

Newsletters. These sources can save a lot of time and trouble by providing information in areas of specific interest. They are also very timely and accurate. The *Education Daily* newsletter is the education community's independent news subscription service. It provides timely, accurate reports of activities in Congress, the U.S. Department of Education, and the White House. It also provides weekly legislative updates, reports on the latest educational research findings and activities, and other newsworthy items. The *Federal Grants and Contracts Weekly,* published every Monday, focuses on opportunities in research, training, and service. A monthly supplement focuses on foundation funding, profiles of key agencies, and updates on new developments, legislation, and regulations. *Education Funding News,* published weekly, provides information on what is happening in Washington and features grant opportunities in the field of education. *Report on Educational Research* provides up-to-date news of breakthrough programs and U.S. studies. It includes coverage of federal research activities, results, and funding. It also reports on testing and evaluation, education reforms, and related topics of interest.

Stage 2: Writing Multiple Grants. Writing multiple grant proposals is as much a science as it is an art. As with most things, content comes before style. It is difficult to obtain just one funded grant proposal, much less carry several at the same time. However, by mastering the system by which grants are awarded, one can successfully apply for several grants at once. Thus, one should be familiar with the key components of a proposal, because without even one of these components, the proposal may not be adequate.

Typical Components of a Grant Proposal. The *introduction,* in which one describes the institution, briefly narrates its history, and establishes its ability to undertake the project under consideration, is extremely important. One should also demonstrate a correlation between the project and the institution's willingness and ability to satisfy the parameters of the grant proposal. Therefore, a brief description of the project should include how the institution believes it can provide a solution to a particular problem and why it can do so better than any other social service or research organization in the community (Plesich, 1989; Smith, 1990; and Brewer, Achilles, and Fuhriman, 1993). The introduction, especially to foundations or corporations, should include the institution's philosophy and goals, its track record with other grant-making agencies, proof of its tax-exempt status, and a brief narrative of the project (Corry, 1986).

The *abstract* should be a clear, concise statement of the proposed project. Since the agency grants officer will probably read the abstract first, one should be sure that it states in precise, interesting language the goals and objectives of the program and methods of achievement. One should also briefly allude to the connection between the interests of the submitting agency and the proposed grantee institution and the nature of the project (Brewer, Achilles, and Fuhriman, 1993). Hall (1988) suggests that the abstract be between 250 and 500 words in length and that it be the last page written.

The *need/problem statement* should be prepared after both formal and informal needs assessments have been undertaken and documented. This process may include the collection of relevant historic, geographic, statistical, and demographic data, as well as studies done by research personnel of local universities and colleges. Literature searches on the project topic should also be included. Lefferts (1990) notes that there are four main ways to "convincingly document need—quantitative documentation; qualitative documentation; documentation of the limitations of existing programs; and documentation of the evidence of demand" (p. 45). Some RFAs put out by federal agencies instruct the applicant to present the need first in the narrative section of the proposal. Readers evaluating the proposal can compare it to others and determine how many points to award to the need section. For example, if one can get up to twenty-five points but if need is not highly convincing, the evaluator may give it only fifteen points. Therefore, it is imperative that one clearly convey the need for the project and include the necessary statistical data. (See the discussion of the issue of proficient staff for needs analysis in Chapter Six.)

One should sufficiently detail the approach, methods, procedures, or plan of operation to be used to accomplish the project objectives and ensure that these methods relate in an obvious way to the desired results. Hall (1988) notes that this section of the proposal is typically the longest part. According to Hall, this section "bears the major burden of telling how the project will be carried out and the rationale for the majority of the budget" (p. 115). Bowker and Associates (1992) suggest that this section of the proposal describe the "activities that will take place in order to achieve the desired results. It is the part of the proposal where the reader should be able to gain a picture in his/her mind of exactly how things work" (p. xix). Overall, this section should describe the activities in detail. One should demonstrate the relationship of each procedure to a stated objective and provide evidence that each procedure has had success in the past. One should show how this project is similar to another successful project or indicate that a specific procedure used before has achieved the desired objective. Each objective should be followed by a plan of action (methods and procedures) for the operational activity that will achieve the objective. One should detail the time line for each activity and indicate the length of time expected for completion of the project (Corry, 1986).

Through examination and articulation of the institution's philosophy and goals and consideration of a clear statement of the problem to be solved, one should arrive at specific program objectives. At this point, writers sometimes confuse goals and objectives. Goals are essentially long-range, broad statements meant to serve the institution for the life of its charter. They will often appear in the letters of incorporation of the institution. An objective, on the other hand, states short-term, specific, realistic, and measurable expectations. Objectives call for precise, measurable results, whereas goals are broad, general statements that cannot be directly measured. Well-written objectives will specify the project's expected results, the length of time needed to achieve these results, and the minimum competency level or service level desired. Hall (1988) notes that goals and objectives usually differ in "dimensions of specificity, accountability and time" (p. 100).

Just as objectives are sometimes confused with goals, writers also tend to substitute procedures or activities for objectives. Objectives say what will be accomplished; procedures or activities tell how it is to be done. A goal might be to provide a specific service to the displaced adult workers of the community. An objective related to that goal might be to enroll one thousand participants in a Displaced Workers Consortium Center by September 30.

The proposed project evaluation must be carefully designed into each objective. If the objective is to close the gap between the current condition of need and a national or regional norm of a service, then the method of evaluation is readily available. However, if the objective is to reach a level of knowledge, skill, or attitude about a service, then an evaluative model must be presented to assess these outcomes. The opinions of the client group will be particularly important in the design of these objectives and the evaluations related to them. The evaluation of the project can determine whether one is reaching one's objectives, and it can provide information that will indicate that adjustments need to be made in the program. Also, an effective evaluation component of the proposal can ascertain what impact was made on adults. Therefore, one should clearly indicate how one plans to measure the degree to which the funded project has achieved its stated objectives and how one will show whether the project was conducted in a manner consistent with the negotiated grant award. In essence, as Lefferts (1990) notes, it is imperative that one be clear about the overall purpose of the evaluation.

Answering the following questions should help one determine whether to include a point in the proposal's evaluation section: Does the evaluation serve to "assess the effectiveness of program methods or approaches? . . . provide funding agencies with a basis for considering refunding or funding additional similar work? . . . meet a legislative requirement? . . . ascertain the effectiveness of one program approach compared to another type of approach aimed at the same problem? . . . be used as a feedback mechanism, so that changes in program methods can be instituted while the project is still going on?" (Lefferts, 1990, p. 64).

The budget for the project should correspond closely to the whole proposal statement. It should be generous enough to allow the institution to perform all the procedures described using the professional personnel needed. It must be specific enough so that no unexplained gross figures appear yet flexible enough so that some room for error is provided. The budget should include anticipated salaries and benefits for the fiscal year in which the project will be completed; operating expenses, including all office supplies, communication expenses, duplication costs, travel, conference fees, and the contract for specific services; equipment such as typewriters and other capital expenditures necessary to the operation of the project; and indirect costs (office space, utilities, administrative costs). Some colleges and universities state that the indirect expenses will be contributed by the institution.

In preparing the budget, one should consult the fiscal officer of the institution as early as possible. As mentioned earlier, one should be generous rather than frugal in estimating costs. After all, it may take several months for the proposal to be prepared, reviewed, signed, submitted, approved, and then implemented. Lastly, one should exercise care in the arithmetic of the budget. It should be checked for accuracy by the fiscal officer of the institution. Careless mistakes and errors can cost the writer a potential grant and result in lost time, effort, and expense. (See Chapter Four's discussion on developing and managing budgets.)

The quality of the personnel who will direct the project should be supplied, with a clear description of how their professional expertise will contribute to the program's objectives. Hall (1988) provides a list of do's in dealing with the personnel section of the proposal: "(1) DO include the title, responsibilities, number and percentage of time assigned to the project for each type of staff person. (2) DO give the names and biographical sketches for staff. (3) DO tailor the biography to emphasize experiences relevant to the project. (4) DO briefly describe the selection process and criteria for key project positions unfilled at the time of application" (p. 152).

Résumés for all persons who will work on the project should be placed in an appendix and highlighted in narrative form in the body of the proposal under experiences on similar programs. The project director's experience with this type of program and his or her fiscal expertise in similar projects should be described. Also, the project director's successful accomplishments in a similar program should be mentioned (Corry, 1986).

Typically, a section on the adequacy of resources shows what institutional resources the applicant plans to devote to the project, including facilities, equipment, and supplies. The funding source wants to be sure that the resources are appropriate and adequate to meet the requirements of the proposal. (See the discussion of external resources in Chapter One, partnerships with "movers" in Chapter Two, and corporate resources in Chapter Nine.)

Appendixes and attachments for supporting data should be used. The program may call for a copy of the school catalogue or IRS tax-exempt data. Important letters of support for the project or other data to strengthen the application may be sent. Appendixes should be used wisely, including only important and related materials. References to all appendixes should be made in the narrative.

This chapter only touches on the typical sections of a grant proposal. However, the RFA or foundation guidelines may require the grant writer to address other major items in the proposal. For example, a federal RFA may require that you provide information on dissemination, impact, or community integration and coordination. The respective grant funders' guidelines should be followed, and information should be provided that is required to make the proposal as complete and competitive as possible.

Grant Writing Tips. In the grant proposal one must convince the grant funder that the project is worth considering and approving. Research and writing skills will have to be the best. Following are some grant-writing tips:

Be realistic; do not promise global changes.
Be factual and specific; do not talk in generalities or in emotional terms. Do not make statements that cannot be substantiated in the proposal.
Explain the need convincingly, and show a connection between needs, goals, objectives, and activities.
Present a proposal for something specific. Do not send in a shopping list, because this, in effect, is asking the funder to determine your priorities. And

do not send in a tome with a request for the funder to "take any portion of it."

Use language for laypeople; avoid unexplained abbreviations, initials, jargon, or verbs turned into nouns (for example, "prioritization").

Use short sentences and the active voice.

Avoid references that are more than five to seven years old unless the reference is considered a classic.

Follow the funding agency's guidelines to a T (Somerville, 1982; Hodge, 1988; Helm, 1990; Brewer, Achilles, and Fuhriman, 1993).

Elements of a Strong Proposal. Proposals that win grants usually contain all of the following elements: (1) a clear and logical connection between needs, goals, objectives, and activities; (2) a plan for documentation and evaluation of the project's progress; (3) a timetable showing where and when each goal, objective, and activity will fall during the project duration; (4) a detailed, realistic budget; (5) a demonstrated familiarity with the literature in the field that is published by the funding agency; (6) a convincing explanation of need for the proposed project—that is, specific names, figures, statistics, problems, and dates to support the claim; (7) details of how project follow-up work is to be accomplished; (8) strict adherence to the guidelines provided by the funding agency; and (9) measurable objectives (Somerville, 1982; Mertens, 1987; Koziol, 1991; Brewer, Achilles, and Fuhriman, 1993). Hall (1988) reports Townsend's "Criteria Grantors Use in Assessing Proposals" findings as to which criteria influenced decisions on funding. The factors that were included in the "very important" category were "purpose, community need, accountability, competence, and feasibility"; factors classified as "important" were "project logic, probable impact, language, money needed, and community support" (p. 185).

Common Proposal Weaknesses. There are pitfalls that can keep proposals from being funded. One should avoid the following common weaknesses: failing to follow proposal guidelines, omitting essential proposal components, or burying components in the text where readers have difficulty locating them; submitting an incomplete or unfinished proposal (make sure every blank is filled); presenting a proposal without a real need; writing proposals that are too lengthy (no one relishes reading a 300-page proposal); trying to reinvent the wheel; and making assumptions about the readers' knowledge of the proposed project (they possess only the information given them) (Helm, 1990; Meador, 1985; Oetting, 1986; Somerville, 1982).

Stage 3: Managing Grants. The grant writer finally has it! The grant award notification or contract is in hand. The administrator will need to be well organized and ready to begin the project soon after receiving the notification; it is common to have less than two months until the start date of the project. One needs to be ready to understand and respond to requirements; organize staff and activities; lead, direct, and control activities, personnel, and finances; communicate and report on performance; control crises and problems; and prepare for re-funding (Lefferts, 1983). (See the discussion of the adult educator as manager of groups in Chapter Five, management functions in Chapter Seven, and management roles in Chapter Ten.)

Initial Implementation Stage. In the start-up phase, after negotiating the grant and while waiting for the arrival of the award letter, one can begin organizing plans for implementation. One will need to consider some of the following areas: staffing (comprehensive descriptions of positions, position announcements); physical requirements (offices and other space needs, phone lines, furniture, office supplies); and record keeping and documentation (fiscal, personnel, and participant records; general files and correspondence; and so forth). Reading and understanding the Education Department General Administration Regulations (EDGAR) Sections 73.730–75.734 will help in record keeping and documentation. A good practice is simply to document *everything* and save copies of everything.

Ongoing Maintenance Stage. If a federal or state grant has been secured, EDGAR plays an important role in the ongoing maintenance stage; these guidelines must be followed. The best way to prepare to operate the project according to the guidelines is to have studied them before beginning to write the proposal. As noted at the beginning of this chapter, writing a proposal is only one component of the grant process; another major component is the actual administration of the funded project. Typically the day-to-day maintenance stage requires the administrator of the grant to manage staff, provide project direction, and continually evaluate management and assessment to ensure the project is fulfilling the overall requirements of the grant.

Assessing Progress. Grant funders like to know how their money is being spent because project success is their success. One should be prepared for site visits or audits. One needs to evaluate the project procedurally and document accomplishments, following the evaluation section included in the proposal narrative. Keeping meticulous records of everything is essential in managing multiple grants. Some funding agencies require maintenance of records for five years or more after the project ends. (See the discussion of role of evaluation in staff development in Chapter Six, collecting evaluation data in Chapter Seven, and preparing for evaluation in Chapter Nine.)

Stage 4: Closing Out Grants. The majority of grants are awarded for a one-year period. However, for grants that are awarded for multiple (three to five) years, the grant award will be made from year to year, with annual performance and financial reporting requirements. Like everything else discussed thus far, closing out a grant requires planning ahead. One should follow the procedures that define financial reporting and assess retention or protection steps that must be taken at the termination of a grant. Grants typically are terminated by the host institution for various reasons. They are terminated by the funder because the grant work has been completed or grant conditions are not met.

Whatever the reason for ending the grant, "the host institution or agency is responsible for closing out the grant as promptly as is feasible after expiration or termination and to ensure that the proper closing procedures are implemented and the assets are divested" (Brewer, Achilles, and Fuhriman, 1993, p. 262). Most federal and state grants require that an annual performance and financial report be submitted within ninety days after completion of the project's program year.

Conclusion

While grants management is of ultimate importance—no money, no projects—another critical component involves the ability to manage the projects well, to build up skills in grant administration. Successful management of grants will improve one's chances of convincing grant funders to keep giving money to fund continuing or future projects. Lefferts (1990) lists the following elements of a program to "ensure that a grant is maintained and renewed: adhering to funder requirements; maintaining positive relationships with funding agencies; implementing an effective program of communications and reporting; assuring effective program and financial management; and preparing a successful reapplication or proposal" (p. 143). The administrator should keep these elements in mind, managing multiple funding sources, writing grant documents, and continuing to explore private and public funding agencies to identify additional sources to help finance and expand the program.

References

Bailey, A. L. "So You Want to Get a Grant." Change, 1990, 17 (1), 40–43.

Bowker, J. J., and Associates. Annual Register of Grant Support: A Directory of Funding Sources. (26th ed.) New Providence, Bahamas: Reed Reference, 1992.

Brewer, E. W., Achilles, C. M., and Fuhriman, J. R. Finding Funding: Grant Writing for the Financially Challenged Educator. Newbury Park, Calif.: Corwin, 1993.

Corry, E. Writing the Effective Grant Proposal. (2nd ed.) Littleton, Colo.: Libraries Unlimited, 1986.

Gelatt, J. P. "Obtaining Grant Funding: Ten Steps to Success." Journal of American Speech and Hearing Association, Feb. 1989, 31, 67–69.

Hall, M. S. Getting Funded: A Complete Guide to Proposal Writing. (3rd ed.) Portland, Oreg.: Continuing Education Publications, 1988.

Helm, B. "Proposal Writing: What About That Fifty-Page Limit?" National Council for Educational Opportunity Associations Journal, Spring 1990, pp. 10–11.

Hodge, W. A. "The Eleven Commandments of Writing Effective Law-Related Education Proposals." The Social Studies, 1988, 79 (1), 4–9.

Koziol, L. C. "Making Your Grant Proposal Work: Some Things Those Grant-Writing Books Never Told You." Pi Lambda Theta Newsletter, 1991, 36 (2), 5–6.

Lefferts, R. The Basic Handbook of Grants Management. New York: Basic Books, 1983.

Lefferts, R. Getting a Grant in the 1990s: How to Write Successful Grant Proposals. New York: Prentice Hall, 1990.

Meador, R. Guidelines for Preparing Proposals. Chelsea, Mich.: Lewis, 1985.

Mertens, T. R. "Reflections on Writing and Reviewing Grant Proposals." Journal of College Science Teaching, Feb. 1987, 16, 267–269.

Oetting, E. R. "Ten Fatal Mistakes in Grant Writing." Professional Psychology, Research and Practice, 1986, 17 (6), 570–573.

Plesich, J. "On Target: How to Write the Grants That Get the Money." Learning, May–June 1989, 17, 38–41.

Reif-Lehrer, L. Writing a Successful Grant Application. (2nd ed.) Boston: Jones and Bartlett, 1989.

Ross, M. "Opportunities for Maximizing the Effectiveness of the Administrator-Researcher Relationship." Journal of the Society of Research Administrators, 1990, 22 (1), 17–22.

Smith, L. C. "Writing Effective Proposals." Business Education Forum, Dec. 1990, 45, 15–16.

Solomon, G. "Where and How to Get Grants." Electronic Learning, 1991, 10 (4), 16–19.

Somerville, B. "Where Proposals Fail." The Grantsmanship Center News, Jan.–Feb. 1982, pp. 24–25.

Sparks, R. D. "Matching Ideas and Funds." Journal of American Speech and Hearing Association, Feb. 1989, 31, 77–99.

Stopka, C. E., and Beland, R. M. "Let's Get Funded: Guidelines for Obtaining Grants." Journal of Physical Education, Recreation, and Dance, Feb. 1989, 60, 67–71.

ERNEST W. BREWER is associate professor and principal investigator and project director in the Department of Technological and Adult Education, College of Education, University of Tennessee, Knoxville. He currently serves as the principal investigator and project director of seven federally funded grants.

Flexible budgeting can be utilized to help coordinate and harmonize the use of scarce financial resources in the adult educational environment.

Developing and Managing Adult Education Budgets

Charles G. Ericksen

Perhaps the most valuable quantitative tool available to an adult education administrator is the budget. Once a budget has been developed, it can be used to manage and control the future financial activity of the organization. A budget is "a financial document created before anticipated transactions occur and is often called a financial plan of action" (Anderson, Needles, and Caldwell, 1989, p. 278). It can also be viewed as a "means of coordinating the combined intelligence of an entire organization into a plan of action" (Rayburn, 1993, p. 296).

The budget is crucial to an effective and efficient organization because it coordinates and harmonizes the utilization of scarce financial resources by comparing actual results against expected outcomes. In addition, budgeting compels adult education administrators to think about the future. This forced planning may well be the major advantage of the budgeting process. (See Chapter Three for a discussion of budgets and grant proposals.)

Types of Budgets

Budgets come in all shapes and sizes and are living documents that are modified and changed as the future unfolds and becomes clearer. They are used by major industrial corporations operating in global markets and by local adult education administrators planning next month's activities. *Master budgets* quantify "management's expectations regarding future income, cash flows, and financial position" (Horngren and Foster, 1991, p. 172). A master budget usually includes operating or annual budgets, capital expenditure budgets for large items, cash budgets, projected income statement budgets, balance sheets, and statements of cash flows. *Short-term operating budgets* are usually developed for twelve-month periods. While long-term operating budgets can be constructed, budgets of longer duration are primarily developed for large capital expenditures. Regardless of the time frame, budgeting should be done on a continual basis to provide management with at least a constant twelve-month forecast. As each month is completed, a new twelfth month is added to take its place.

Adult educators may find the short-term operating budget the most useful because it allows one to monitor the pulse of the program on a day-to-day basis. The short-term, day-to-day operating budget will usually include at least an income and expense budget for the next twelve months. The amount of detail contained in the operating budget usually depends on the program size and need for timely, relevant information. Obviously, financial requirements and practices vary widely, since some programs are completely subsidized and others must show a profit (Knowles, 1980). In budgeting, as in most other activities, a proper balance must be attained between too much detail and not enough. Needless to say, once this golden mean is obtained, a program will have the potential to operate at its most effective and efficient financial point.

An operating budget projecting income is usually developed first because operating expenditures are likely to be directly or indirectly related to the forecasted income. Once forecasted income is determined, the operating budget simply falls into place. However, determining forecasted income may turn out to be one of the hardest tasks in the budgeting process. Course income or revenue "is usually the easiest course budget element to calculate and the most difficult to estimate" (Matkin, 1985, p. 32). Economists simply assume that demand will exist at a specified level, but in the real world, it turns out to be much more complicated.

Generally, the next year's income projection is based at least loosely on the current year's income, but before a final figure is determined, many other factors need to be considered, for example, the general economic condition of the country, pricing policies of the organization, available advertising, competition, seasonal variations, economic cycles, population shifts, and unemployment in the general geographic area. It may even be desirable to use complicated statistical methods such as econometrics (a statistical tool that measures national output and income using probability theory) or correlational analysis to do "what if" analysis before the income budget process is completed. In the final analysis, however, most administrators use the aforementioned factors and their professional judgment to derive an income projection around which to build their operating expenditures. Although the procedures for building these projections are still crude, this must not deter skillful guesswork based on information, insights, and shrewd speculation (Keller, 1983).

Once a forecasted income has been developed, the clerical support, fringe benefits, instructional staff, travel, course materials, room rentals, entertainment, janitorial, and miscellaneous expenses can be estimated. Thus, the income projection is the key to the entire operating budget process because it drives total expenditures. It is indeed unfortunate that a crystal ball cannot be used to determine future participation in adult educational programs.

Fixed Budgets

A fixed or static budget "estimates costs for a single activity volume" and is not adjusted when actual volume differs (Rayburn, 1993, p. 301). A fixed budget is ideal when it coincides with the forecasted income level. However, if actual income is different from the forecasted income, then the fixed budget may be of little use to an administrator because it compares apples to oranges. For example, if projected income is $4,000 and actual income turns out to be $5,900, the fixed budget reveals only that a variance exists from the original targeted income. It does not provide an indication of how efficiently specific expenditures were utilized. The major advantage of fixed budgeting is its simplicity. The disadvantages outweigh the advantages, however, since a fixed budget will almost always create a variance that is difficult to understand when comparing actual performance to budgeted performance in the aggregate.

Flexible Budgets

A flexible budget takes into account a wide variety of income levels and can be developed for one program participant or one million participants. A flexible budget provides a "summary of anticipated costs prepared for a range of different activity levels" (Anderson, Needles, and Caldwell, 1989, p. G-4). To develop a flexible budget, prior knowledge about cost behavior is needed.

Generally speaking, expenditures are either fixed or variable over a certain relevant range of activity. Fixed costs remain constant in total amount within this range of activity. The program director's salary would be an example of a fixed cost. On the other hand, variable costs such as course materials change in total in direct proportion to the activity. Variable costs put the "flex" into flexible budgeting. Flexible operating budgets allow a suitable comparison of actual expenditures with estimated expenditures at the same activity or income level. For example, if an additional $4,000 was spent on course supplies over what was budgeted at the same activity level, then an administrator has something concrete on which to focus. The $4,000 difference could reflect waste of material at various course locations, or it might simply reflect the fact that suppliers' prices have gone up substantially. Either way, action can be taken to bring the expenditure into alignment with the budget. The variance simply calls attention to an area that may need further analysis to maintain financial efficiency.

A flexible budget is perhaps the most beneficial financial tool available to program administrators involved in day-to-day activities because it isolates income and expense variances. A typical flexible budget for various volume levels appears in Table 4.1.

Once actual performance has been determined, actual and flexible budget amounts at the same volume level can be compared. The advantage of using this format is the focus placed on the numerous variances. A flexible budget with variances appears in Table 4.2.

Table 4.1. A Sample Flexible Budget

	Budget per Participant	Volume Level		
Number of participants		100	120	140
Income	180	$18,000	$21,600	$25,200
Variable costs				
Supplies	20	2,000	2,400	2,800
Refreshments	15	1,500	1,800	2,100
Computer use	10	1,000	1,200	1,400
Fixed costs				
Instruction		6,000	6,000	6,000
Building rental		500	500	500
Total costs		11,000	11,900	12,800
Profit		7,000	9,700	12,400

Table 4.2. A Sample Flexible Budget with Variances

	Budget per Participant	Budget Volume	Actual Volume	Variance
Number of participants		120	120	
Income	$180	$21,600	$17,200	$4,300U[a]
Variable costs				
Supplies	20	2,400	2,900	500U
Refreshments	15	1,800	2,000	200U
Computer time	10	1,200	1,000	200F
Fixed costs				
Instruction		6,000	6,000	200U
Building rental		500	500	0
Total cost		11,900	12,600	700U
Profit		$9,700	$4,600	$5,100U

[a] U = unfavorable; F = favorable.

Unfavorable expense variances are created when actual expenditures exceed what has been forecasted. *Favorable expense variances* result when actual expenditures are less than expected. A variance simply means that income was more or less than forecasted. Comparison and further analysis of the prior example may indicate that income was less than expected because course fees were reduced to stimulate local interest in the course. In addition, the course materials might have been unfavorable because the orders were placed too late with the supplier. Perhaps the refreshments had to be increased because the course was scheduled at dinnertime. Computer time may have had a favorable variance because the participants had to drive a substantial distance to attend the course and therefore left early. Finally, instructional costs may have been more than anticipated because a last-minute replacement had to be used in place of the usual instructor.

A plethora of reasons may explain why the variances existed. However, without the flexible budget it would be impossible to know whether the actual situation was good or bad. The flexible budget established a standard that could subsequently be utilized for corrective action. Flexible budgeting allows management to forecast a variety of scenarios so future strategies can be prepared and implemented if necessary (Mannino and Milani, 1992).

Break-Even Analysis

An adult educator may find it informative to know how many participants are needed to break even on a course offering. In the previous example, recall that the course fee was $180 and that the variable costs per participant were $45. By simply dividing the total fixed cost by the difference between total income per participant and variable cost per participant one can determine the course break-even point. This is the exact point where the course generates no profit or loss. This calculation is made as follows:

Participant course fee	$180
Participant variable cost	45
Difference	$135

Total fixed costs $6,500 / $135 difference = 48 participants

It appears that the current course offering will break even with forty-eight participants at the $180 fee. Therefore, if final enrollment is less than forty-eight participants, the course will be operating at a loss. Because many adult education programs are now dealing with the harsh realities of fewer dollars, an offering that produces a loss will need to be seriously reevaluated before it is allowed to proceed, because too many course losses could affect the viability of an entire program.

Multidimensional Budgeting

Conventional budgeting can provide tremendous insight into a program's financial capability, but recent findings suggest that this perception can be further enhanced. For example, a technique called multidimensional budgeting (MDB) can supplement traditional budgeting and help provide higher profitability and an improved competitive position. It primarily "focuses on the relationships between spending and the underlying value created, rather than merely how budgeted funds are spent" (Schmidt, 1992, p. 104). The evolution of MDB suggests that budgeting research will continue to further refine and define itself in an effort to make organizations more efficient and responsive to domestic and global competition.

Conclusion

With fewer dollars flowing into education, the adult education administrator can expect to be held more accountable for the *financial stewardship* of programs. The budgeting technique presented in this chapter simply provides one tool for planning and controlling adult education programs in an ever-changing environment. In addition to budgeting, advanced knowledge of management, marketing, economics, accounting, and finance will probably be required. The adult education administrators of the future will need to understand planning, organizing, controlling, directing, staffing, motivating, and communicating as well as they understand basic adult learning theory and participation.

A number of financial tools are available to assist the adult administrator with program planning and control. Perhaps the most useful tool is the flexible budget. The flexible budget allows the program director to plan for different activity levels while isolating variances. Variance isolation permits one to manage by exception. In other words, more of the program director's time and effort can be spent trying to understand and modify unusual occurrences.

The flexible budget, along with the cash budget and capital budget, is one of the many types of budgets available to help the program director stay on course. In the future, in addition to the aforementioned budgets, new approaches such as MDB will be available for use in the adult education environment. The adult education administrator will be dealing with an environment that is more complex and that will need the services of someone well versed in finance, management, and marketing. The administrator who is knowledgeable, proactive, and adaptable will no doubt seize the day.

References

Anderson, H. R., Needles, B. E., and Caldwell, J. C. *Management Accounting*. Boston: Houghton Mifflin, 1989.

Horngren, C. T., and Foster, G. *Cost Accounting: A Managerial Emphasis*. Englewood Cliffs, N.J.: Prentice Hall, 1991.

Keller, G. *Academic Strategy: The Management Revolution in American Higher Education*. Baltimore: Johns Hopkins University Press, 1983.

Knowles, M. S. *The Modern Practice of Adult Education: From Pedagogy to Andragogy*. Chicago: Follett, 1980.

Mannino, P. V., and Milani, K. "Budgeting for an International Business." *Management Accounting,* 1992, 73 (8), 36–41.

Matkin, G. W. *Effective Budgeting in Continuing Education*. San Francisco: Jossey-Bass, 1985.

Rayburn, L. G. *Cost Accounting: Using a Cost Management Approach*. Boston: Irwin, 1993.

Schmidt, J. A. "Is It Time to Replace Traditional Budgeting?" *Journal of Accountancy,* 1992, 174 (4), 103–107

CHARLES G. ERICKSEN is associate professor of accounting, business, and economics at Carroll College in Helena, Montana. He has held various administrative positions at the postsecondary level.

Working with groups is an effective way to build adult education programs, expand services, and strengthen community ties. Involving groups requires advanced planning, strong communication systems, and excellent problem-solving skills.

Utilizing Unilateral and Multilateral Groups to Enhance Program Development

Mary S. Charuhas

The purpose of this chapter is to provide a framework for the utilization of groups in adult education program management that allows administrators to consider the various qualities of groups, to evaluate and select those qualities most appropriate for their programmatic needs, and to integrate group management into their own program operations. First, a rationale for working with groups is presented. Second, a framework for characterizing various groups is provided. Third, different types of groups are described and illustrated in an educational setting.

Rationale for Utilizing Groups

Working in conjunction with the community through various kinds of groups has been identified as one of the standards for judging program quality (Association of Community Based Education, 1983; Towey, 1985) and listed as one of the key components of program excellence in surveys of successful adult education programs (Houston Read Commission, 1989; Decker and Romney, 1990; Kutner, Furey, Webb, and Gadsen, 1990). Smith and Offerman (1990), Montreal Catholic School Commission (1989), and the California Department of Education (1989) recommend it as an effective means of working with diverse populations. The California Department of Education (1989) proposes it as a means of improving planning. Carl Perkins' legislation and other federal guides (Olivia, 1988; Hickey, 1986) incorporate coordination into their funding regulations. Amstutz (1992) recognizes group coordination as a means of conserving resources. Heaney (1992) identifies it as a strategy community-based organizations can use to protect themselves from the complex bureaucratic demands of government agencies. Guglielmino, Frock, and Burrichter (1988) cite collaborative skills as one of the principal competencies of successful adult education administrators. Whether gathering information for planning and evaluation purposes, seeking the means to conserve resources while simultaneously increasing services, or reaching out to support community, the ability of administrators to work with groups in a constructive and wholly integrated manner will result in increased communication, enhanced understanding of their community, and improved programming (Olivia, 1988).

Educational institutions no longer have the luxury of operating independently from their communities. Expertise in education is no longer sufficient for the maintenance or continuation of a program. As state and federal funding decline and resources become scarce, taxpayers question the costs and carefully weigh the benefits of the community services provided by adult education departments. (See the discussion of external resources for program development in Chapter One and grant administration in Chapter Three.) They scrutinize the need for some of these programs and the value of others. They recognize the proliferation of governmental and social agencies that has resulted in duplication of services and ask which institutions can best do the job. The resulting competition has led to more demands for tighter budgets and, simultaneously, expectations for greater service (McClenney and Mingle, 1992). (See the definition of accountability in Chapter One and alternative accountability models in Chapter Nine.)

To be competitive, the adult continuing education administrator must have current and accurate information about the community (Hand and Sellen, 1979). Programs cannot be designed solely on the basis of statistical reports. Demographics alone do not reflect the values or cultural priorities of the community. Community representatives on focus groups, task forces, and advisory bodies can enrich the data, offer new perspectives on programming, and encourage more people to have a stake in the success of programs.

Even competitors can benefit from collaborative efforts. To remain competitive, a program must reduce costs and increase revenue. Through collaborative planning, participants can better define their missions, client populations, and their geographic boundaries. This can result in the participants designing more efficient systems for themselves. By identifying their mutual problems, they derive common solutions without losing individual integrity. Formalizing these collaborative efforts results in teams of agencies that can jointly apply for funding or pool resources, including staff and facilities.

Stimulating demand is a third way to remain competitive. Working with groups is effective there as well. Supporting and nurturing small community-based organizations to allow them to become self-sufficient will eventually result in their becoming new client groups for larger, more formal education institutions.

Education leaders have an important responsibility to apprise the community of the policies, goals, and procedures of their respective organizations. When instructional, curricular, and administrative philosophies are explained and program issues are clarified, public support for expenditures and commitment to program goals can be secured. When policies and procedures are subjected to public scrutiny, discussions can take place that lead to policy changes congruent with the needs of the community. The ensuing dialogue can clarify the criteria used to provide evidence of quality, productivity, and accountability. If understanding and consensus are reached through dialogue, members of the group may then become advocates and support adult education programs.

Framework for Characterizing Groups

Trutko and others (1991) note that groups vary in terms of their initiators, numbers of agencies involved, and degrees of coordination. Hickey (1986) distinguishes groups in a model of concentric circles moving from collaboration (groups that only work together), to cooperation (groups that form an association for common benefit), to coordination (groups that work toward effective results), and finally centering on the target: program outcomes. This model is affected by multiple societal forces portrayed as arrows pointing to the concentric circles. Common to both models is the degree of involvement the participants have in accomplishing goals. In addition, both authors agree that the terms in both research and practice that refer to these groups have been used interchangeably (Trutko and others, 1991; Hickey, 1986).

Recognizing the contributions of these two models, it is important to expand on the qualities that differentiate groups. The first quality of a group to be considered is *complexity*. In a unilateral group, the product or outcome of the group's work is directed toward one agency. Multilateral groups are established among several agencies to achieve a common goal through mutual benefit (Gold, 1988). The second quality is the *freedom to participate* in the group, or obligation—whether participation is voluntary, encouraged, or mandated by legislation or a funding source. The third quality is the *degree of commitment,* ranging from simple attendance, to verbal commitments, to legally binding contracts. *Locus of control,* the fourth quality, refers to the group's power in relationship to the adult educator. The fifth quality is the expected and actual *duration* of the group and length of terms of office. The sixth quality focuses on the *goals* of the group. The goals may be targeted to accomplish one specific goal or may be comprehensive, encompassing major societal changes. The last quality refers to the *degree of integration.* At one extreme, the members of the group operate completely independently, sharing only minimal information. At the other extreme, the group becomes so integrated that it becomes an independent unit that can act on its own.

Next in the discussion is a brief description of external groups. The description, categorized by complexity, highlights other qualities. The list of groups is designed to provide a range of group responsibility and organizational impact.

Unilateral Groups

Focus groups, task forces, and advisory committees, councils, or boards are formed by the adult education administrator to access needed information about changing demographics, economics, politics, and attitudes of a community toward an organization. A strong network consisting of educational, community, political, business, and industrial representatives providing information is a critical factor in the management of any program. The information this dialogue provides may then be used in all aspects of the program management process, including strategic planning, quality design, productivity analysis, accountability reports, and formative and summative evaluation. Some definitions of groups are available in marketing literature. For purposes of this chapter, groups will be defined as follows according to my experience.

Focus groups are small formal or informal groups of representatives selected often randomly from a designated population at a time when modification of an operation is possible. These groups are asked to identify issues regarding their particular relationship to an adult education department. Focus groups are managed by the adult continuing education administrator, are voluntary, and are usually very limited in scope. They have limited control and rarely meet more than once. For example, at one urban educational institution a random sample of African American students was asked to evaluate a recruitment strategy. Discussions resulted in scheduling additional classes in late afternoon so that parents could take a class after work and still be able to pick up their children.

Task forces are created by the adult education administrator to clarify issues and establish a plan of action to solve a community problem when both community support is needed and a variety of options are available. Though longer in duration than focus groups, they are still limited in scope. The representatives are selected because they have expertise on the task force issue and the authority within the community to ensure the task force's success. They are expected to recommend a plan of action but also to support its implementation by the adult education administrator; this makes it more complex. Membership is voluntary, but commitment is much higher than in a focus group; however, it usually is not legally binding. Because the group is expected to do much more than discuss issues, it has much more control. An example of a task force was that created by an agency faced with determining the most effective way to serve the immediate and long-term needs of pregnant teenage girls. The task force was able to achieve the support of high school counselors, create a referral system, and raise money.

Advisory committees, councils, or boards are long-term systems that are designed to systematically and continually direct information into an organization. Consisting usually of voluntary representative members of the department's client group or all affected agencies, this group needs to be committed to the long-term growth of the department and the accomplishment of its goals. Responsible for examining broad-based issues in the adult education department, this formal group is used at all stages of program management. Simultaneously, the advisory body is learning about the agency, and the commitment to the program is high. Because it is long term, the advisory body has more influence or control than a task force. An example of an advisory body involves an agency responsible for serving a large geographic area. The agency wanted to assure each district that its needs would be met. A student representative, political leader, a businessperson, and a district community leader examined access, recruitment, retention policies, and success rates by economic, ethnic, and racial populations. Analysis was used to develop strategic plans, modify programs and operations, and evaluate the strengths and weaknesses of the department.

Multilateral groups or coalitions, cooperatives, and alliances refer to groups of peer agencies external to the adult education department. Adult education administrators may choose to participate in already existing coordination groups or create their own. In either case, their existence is based on a mutual interest or need to achieve a common goal or solve a common problem.

Low-Obligation Multilateral Groups

Coalitions, the most generic term used to refer to groups, is used here to discuss short-term, single-purpose groups of different agencies that formally or informally come together for a brief time to achieve a specific purpose. Because many adult education departments operate on restricted funding, they are dependent on part-time instructional staff, word-of-mouth advertising, and limited staff development. By participating with a group of agencies to coordinate efforts, however, the adult education director can combine resources to accomplish in a coalition what could not be accomplished alone. Control is shared, commitments are limited to specific tasks, and agreements may or may not be formalized in minutes or letters of understanding. A coalition is exemplified by groups of agencies serving the Hispanic community that were faced with the expense of recruiting a large number of students in a short period of time. The media coverage available covered a wide geographic area, and advertising was very expensive. Several agencies formed a coalition to design an ad that listed contact people by geographic area. The coalition created a simple reference system to refer any misdirected phone calls and shared the costs.

Community cooperatives often develop voluntarily when agency directors acknowledge the need for cooperation and coordination with other agencies to provide a system of services to their clients. By designing a joint project, the related agencies can provide comprehensive services, thereby creating a greater opportunity to effect change. For this to function on a continuing basis, the multilateral group would have to have a deep sense of ownership of the process. It would require high commitment and integration, especially where personnel and funds were concerned. For example, four community agencies were teaching job search skills to public aid recipients. All four were marginal programs, and each required staff members to fill several job responsibilities. A discussion resulted in the decision that each agency would focus on the services (that is, recruitment, instruction, support services, and job placement) that it was most qualified to provide, and all shared the client base. All four agencies were able to double the number of clients served and still meet the funding source criteria for success.

Consortia give various groups the opportunity to work in unison to accomplish a single task. Centralizing an activity such as purchasing office supplies and equipment allows agencies to benefit from the discounts given with quantity orders. This group, because of the fiscal and contractual concerns, has high commitment and moderately high integration of services. An example of a consortium involves several adult education agencies that felt they wanted their staff members to learn more about cross-cultural communication. Individually they could not afford to send all their staff members for training; instead, they combined funds to pay for a presenter for a local workshop on the topic. This significantly reduced travel costs and gave staff members the opportunity to meet professionally.

Alliances are generally the broadest in scope of the peer agency function. The members are the leaders of the community who make a long-term public commitment of resources and staff to effect a change in the community. Because an alliance reflects a public commitment to a given issue, it will be held to a public evaluation. This high-commitment group may or may not have contractual agreements, but because of the public visibility, group members will have moderately strong commitments to the project.

An example of an alliance of political, social, community, educational, and governmental leaders relates to an alarming increase in gang activity in a community. Leaders who joined together to make a public commitment and combine resources to fight gangs included the mayor of the city; the chief of police; a corporation president; a dean of adult and community education; the directors of public aid, Job Training Partnership Act, public housing, and state employment services; and the regional superintendent of schools. The members made fighting gangs a priority within their respective agencies, committing both staff and funds to support the effort.

High-Obligation Multilateral Groups

Subcontracts, partnerships, planning councils, and other self-regulatory groups exist primarily as a result of legal, fiscal, or contractual requirements. Their creation could be the result of mandated coordination of services as stipulated by a funding source or a contractual arrangement among agencies. Contractual arrangements are usually made whenever funding, especially tax dollars, and personnel issues must be clarified. When these issues arise, even the most casual of coalitions may move into the high-obligation category. In this situation, integration of services, target goals, and duration of effort is usually specified in formal agreements among the members.

Partnerships are more formal and for a longer term than coalitions or consortia. They operate as a unit, with all members being responsible for the actions the partnership takes. For example, in one community several adult education programs were offered small literacy volunteer start-up grants. With the limits placed on administrative record-keeping costs, the directors were not interested in applying for the funds. When five agencies created a consortium and applied for the funding as a unit, however, there was enough money to cover the costs of staff necessary to provide recruitment, training, and placement of volunteers, as well as testing, placing, and tutoring of students for all five agencies. The partnership then served as a buffer between the adult education agencies and the demands of the funding source. Though the staff members were actually employed by one of the institutions, they were integrated to the point that they were recognized as an independent agency that was able to seek funds from other sources.

Subcontracts are formed for a variety of reasons, but mainly when agreements and understandings must be specified for operational or auditing purposes. The contractor is responsible and accountable for the subcontractor and consequently has some level of administrative control over the subcontractor. Improperly designed, this arrangement can have a stifling effect on the subcontractor, resulting in loss of independence and control. If negotiated, the contract can, on the other hand, clarify initially most of the control issues and identify areas of freedom of action.

Since no one institution is capable of serving all the needs of a community, it is to the benefit of the contractor to arrange for services (such as, housing advocacy) for its clients through other agencies. Those agencies serving populations that may not have access to larger, more formal educational systems can benefit by arranging help for their clients to make the transition to more advanced training. In the end, both agencies can receive maximum benefit from the relationship.

An example of a subcontract involves a community-based organization (CBO) located in a high-risk multiethnic neighborhood. The CBO provided literacy services along with advocacy support for employment, housing, and health, but the CBO could not access public funds for their literacy effort. The CBO subcontracted with the local community college to acquire the necessary funds; in return, the CBO transferred its advanced students into college programs, which thereby improved the minority recruitment efforts of the college. In addition, the graduates of the CBO's clerical skills programs were eligible to apply for secretarial positions at the college, which resulted in the college's acquisition of additional multilingual staff. The CBO's faculty participated in college staff development activities that broadened everyone's understanding of cultural diversity. The CBO even raised private funds to cover a substantial portion of a community-wide staff development conference.

Planning councils. State laws and various funding sources now mandate that groups of peer organizations regularly meet to prevent the duplication of services and ineffective use of local, state, and federal funds. Groups of this nature are often self-governing. Faced with fiscal or legal penalties for failure to arrive at a satisfactory agreement of providers and locations, agencies may consider successful participation in these groups to be essential. This is a high-obligation type of group. Control may rest within the group itself or with the legal manager of the funding source. For example, Illinois agencies that receive state funding for adult education programs and that are located in specified community college districts are mandated to meet and to submit a single operational plan that shows evidence of coordination of services. The quality of the plan and the evidence of nonduplication of services has a direct effect on the funding provided to the participating agencies.

Any one of the groups described in this chapter may take on various functions at various times. A planning council may take on the responsibility of an alliance, or a coalition may choose to formalize into a consortium. People functioning together will shift in purpose and direction as need and personalities direct them.

The Adult Continuing Education Administrator's Role in Managing Groups

Gold (1988, pp. 32–33) describes the various, multiple, or changing roles the adult continuing education administrator can have in relationship to the members of the group. In the *buffer* role, a person is responsible for identifying the interest, initiating contact, and maintaining contacts with the establishing agency. As the *broker,* one negotiates among the participants to identify mutual areas of concern or intervenes in the participants' activities to break down barriers preventing the group formation. In the role of *catalyst,* a person may not even be an active participant but provides the energy to make the group coalesce. As a *facilitator,* an individual assists the participants in accomplishing their goals. Lastly, in the *manager* role, a person is charged by the group to direct the decision-making process. To this list, one could add the role of *participant*. This individual's responsibility is to be involved, contribute, negotiate, collaborate, cooperate, or coordinate with the other members of the group. (See the discussion of managing multiple grants in Chapter Three, management functions in Chapter Seven, and management roles in Chapter Ten.)

For the director who is creating a group, the selection of its members should be done thoughtfully. Since one person is rarely able to identify all the people, agencies, and organizations that should be involved, those people who have a stake in the result of the group's formation should be invited to assist with the selection. In one, or at most two, meetings, stakeholders should do the following:

Finalize the rationale for establishing the group and its purpose.
Identify the populations that should be represented by the group and why.
Identify those who should not be represented by the group and why.
Anticipate both the desirable and undesirable consequences of creating the group.
Devise a strategy for identifying actual members. (See the discussion of involving the stakeholder in Chapter Eight, higher education stakeholders in Chapter Nine, and the humanistic administrator in Chapter Ten).

This seemingly more cumbersome two-step process is one that will build understanding and, later, acceptance of the group's activities. For administrators who are joining a group rather than establishing one, the concerns listed here are the same. Instead of designing the criteria, the administrator compares the criteria to the established mission, goals, existing membership, and established outcomes of the group.

Communication Systems Revisited

All external contact with the community generates information, which must be used in making the decisions necessary to improve education. Information becomes meaningful only when the people affected have the opportunity to debate, assimilate, and accommodate or reject it. Just as information acquired from the group must move through the adult education department and to the parent organization, the consequences of the group's input must be communicated back to the group (Drucker, 1992). It is a message to the group that what they do is important. In addition, conveying the accomplishments of the group to the public is important. It reinforces the continuation of the group's activities. Those members who care will be recognized. More importantly, the community itself will be reminded that the group is acting on the community's behalf.

There are times when, instead of assimilation and accommodation to the activities or recommendations of the group, the administrator must reject the group's proposals. Outright rejection of the actions of a group will be interpreted as though the members of the group themselves have been rejected. This can have long-term negative effects on those individuals and the agencies and institutions they represent (Peters, 1987). If the information is rejected, particularly in unilateral groups, then an overwhelming amount of evidence must be brought forward to the group to provide them with the information they will need to counter their already-held beliefs. The countering information must convince not only the members of the group but also the vast network of people with whom the members of that group function. For that reason alone, the more the members of the group know about each other's operations, the more constructive their recommendations will be and the less likely any one member of the group will be angrily confronted.

Therefore, everything possible must be done to help the group be informed and make knowledgeable decisions. Group development, then, is the critical factor in the successful integration of groups into a management system. For groups to develop fully, they must have continual opportunities for learning everything. Groups must learn about the adult education department, its peer departments, and its parent organization. Groups must understand the mission, goals, operational procedures, regulatory and budgetary constraints, and staffs of the institution they advise.

Then the members must learn about each other, who or what they represent, what they each think is important and why, what they hope to accomplish, and how they benefit from being in the group. They must learn about the community and the clients and evaluate whether as a group they, in fact, represent them. They must learn problem-solving skills and information analysis. They need to understand how to negotiate and how to plan. In unilateral groups, the members must understand financial, legal, and operational limitations of the adult education department. In multilateral groups, everyone must explain his or her own system to the others. In addition, groups working together in high-obligation arrangements must understand the agencies that impose the laws and the contracts that bind them as well. It is a dynamic process, which repeats itself in a new way each time a new member joins. (See also the discussion of telecommunications in Chapter Seven.)

Conclusion: Building Strong Relationships

Collaborative relationships are fragile and take time and hard work. Each party must be clear about needs to be met and goals to be attained. Self-actualization is important because the group needs a sense of accomplishment to give meaning to its existence. From the very first meeting, systems must be designed for decision making, task assignments, management responsibility, and problem solving. Fundamentally, this is the process of building strong relationships (Kasworm, Shoopman, and Dahlin-Brown, 1990; Drucker, 1992; Fisher and Brown, 1988). Compromise, consensus, negotiation, and collaboration are various terms for the process of reaching an agreement. The differences are subtle but can have profound effects on the development of the group.

Majority rule is the most common method of coming to a decision, but it or a less formal form, consensus, becomes domination when the members of the majority and minority never fluctuate. Compromise is the settling of differences by making concessions. The members of the group focus on their assets and goals, giving them away one by one until an agreement is reached. With this method all participants feel that they have lost something. Negotiation, the arrangement of terms through discussion, is dealing or trading one resource for another. This process again requires people to look out for their own needs, often at the expense of others. Collaboration, a process of working together, focuses on the process of building a relationship.

Cooperation and, finally, coordination cannot take place until a common goal has been identified and mutual benefit defined. If the membership has agreed on the goals for mutual benefit, then even those who have given up something will feel that achieving the goal will more than compensate for any concessions made. The debate and negotiation that take place as people agree to work out their difficulties in a meaningful way actually strengthen the group. The synergy that develops as a team of people work together exceeds the accomplishments of individuals acting alone. Working alone isolates not only adult educators but clients as well. It makes it that much more difficult for them to access services to enable them to become self-supporting. This chapter has referred to the kinds of collaborative efforts that can be done locally. Policy makers now need to design eligibility, funding, administrative, and reporting systems that are compatible with the concept of collaboration.

Community and institutional integration is effective because the benefits derived from clear communication with the public will improve the quality of program planning. Coordinating resources will not only improve services to the community but actually increase the quantity and quality of the resources available. Facilitating the growth of community independence will increase not further competition, but rather the need for even more services. Exploring new perspectives on learning will give us new insight into our own programs.

References

Amstutz, D. "Managing Limited Resources: Entrepreneurs in Higher Education." Adult Learning, 1992, 3 (5), 7–9.

Association of Community Based Education. Standards of Performance for Community Based Educational Institutions. Washington, D.C.: Association of Community Based Education, 1983.

California Department of Education. Adult Education for the 21st Century: Strategic Plan to Meet California's Long-Term Adult Education Needs. Sacramento: California Department of Education Youth, Adult, and Alternative Educational Services Division, 1989.

Decker, L. E., and Romney, V. A. Community Education Across America. Profiles of State Networks and Local Projects. Charlottesville: MidAtlantic Center for Community Education, Virginia University, 1990.

Drucker, P. F. Managing for the Future: The 1990s and Beyond. New York: Truman M. Talley Books, 1992.

Fisher, R., and Brown, S. Getting Together: Building Relationships as We Negotiate. New York: Penguin Books, 1988.

Gold, G. G. Improving Community Collaboration for Adult Literacy Programs in Maryland: A Training Guide. Washington, D.C.: National Institute for Work and Learning, 1988.

Guglielmino, L. M., Frock, T., and Burrichter, A. W. The Adult Community Education Administrator Position: A Job Analysis. Boca Raton: Florida Atlantic University, Adult Education Division, 1988.

Hand, S., and Sellen, J. "Program Coordination, Cooperation, and Interorganizational Systems at the Community Level." In Managing Adult Education Programs and Staff. Washington, D.C.: American Association for Adult and Continuing Education, 1979.

Heaney, T. "Resources for Popular Education." *Adult Learning,* 1992, *3* (5), 10–11.

Hickey, D. L. *Collaboration, Cooperation, and Coordination Toward a Definition for Educators and Job Trainers: A Case Study Approach.* Columbus: National Center for Research in Vocational Education, Ohio State University, 1986.

Houston Read Commission. *Profiles of Neighborhood Learning Centers Demonstration and Pilot Projects Operated by the Houston Read Commission in Cooperation with Organizations and Individuals in the Private, Public, and Volunteer Sectors.* Houston: Houston Read Commission, 1989.

Kasworm, C., Shoopman, C., and Dahlin-Brown, N. "Cooperation: A Win-Win Approach to Continuing Education." In *Education for a Multicultural Society: A New Agenda for Continuing Higher Education. Proceedings of the Annual Meeting.* Charleston, S.C.: Association for Adult Continuing Education, 1990.

Kutner, M. A., Furey, S., Webb, L., and Gadsen, V. *Adult Education Programs and Services: A View from Nine Programs.* Washington, D.C.: Pelavin Associates, 1990.

McClenney, K., and Mingle, J. "Higher Education Finance in the 1990s: Hard Choices for Community Colleges," *Leadership Abstracts,* 1992, *5* (7).

Montreal Catholic School Commission. *Profile of a Quality Centre.* Quebec, Canada: Montreal Catholic School Commission, 1989.

Olivia, J. "Interagency Involvement." In *Promoting Adult Learning: Approaches to Literacy, ESL, and Parental Involvement. Proceedings of the Annual Symposium (2nd, Miami, Florida, June 11–12, 1987.* Miami: College of Education, Florida International University, 1988.

Peters, T. J. *Thriving on Chaos: Handbook for a Management Revolution.* New York: Knopf, 1987.

Smith, D. H., and Offerman, M. J. "The Management of Adult Continuing Education." In S. B. Merriam and P. M. Cunningham (eds.), *Handbook of Adult and Continuing Education.* San Francisco: Jossey-Bass, 1990.

Towey, C. F. *Quality Standards for Adult Education Programs.* Washington, D.C.: U.S. Department of Education, 1985. (ED 263 338)

Trutko, J., and others. *An Assessment of JTPA Role in State and Local Coordination Activities.* Research and Evaluation Report Series 91-D. Arlington, Va.: Bell and Associates, Inc., 1991.

MARY S. CHARUHAS is associate dean, Adult Continuing Education and Extension Services, College of Lake County, Grayslake, Illinois.

Many areas of adult education utilize great numbers of part-time instructors with a range of experience. These factors, as well as high staff turnover and complex teaching demands, contribute to the increasingly significant and prominent roles that staff development plays in adult education.

Developing Effective Staff Development Programs

Dennis Terdy

Systematic attention to the field of adult education staff development is relatively recent, as staff development has been termed "a surprisingly neglected consideration" (Knox, 1991, p. 236). Jones's (1991) findings that "there is no systematic body of knowledge pertaining specifically to Adult Basic Education staff development practices" might aptly apply to adult education staff development in general (p. 2). When knowledge regarding staff development is available, it is likely to be embedded in broader topics such as leadership, staffing, or personnel policies and selection; applications may also be drawn from continuing professional education and organizational development (Knox, 1991).

A variety of delivery systems are currently being used to deliver staff development. These include local program-sponsored activities, regional activities, state or national conferences, graduate programs, internships, consultations, and sabbatical leaves (Strother and Klus, 1982). In addition, professional literature, data bases, and clearinghouses also can serve as resources for staff development.

Funding and resources are often cited as primary staff development program components; however, they represent a small contribution to the implementation of an effective staff development program. Jones (1991) indicates, "Meaningful and lasting change requires an established staff development program with clearly defined procedures, long-range goals, and carefully constructed support systems" (p. 13). These characteristics are often missing from the most established adult education training programs. (See the discussion of literacy issues in Chapter One and literacy as a metaphor for adult education in Chapter Two.)

NEW DIRECTIONS FOR ADULT AND CONTINUING EDUCATION, no. 60, Winter 1993 © Jossey-Bass Publishers

In the introduction to "State of the Art in Inservice Education" Cooper and Jones (1984) note that the literature of staff development lacks consensus as to the best means of allocating available resources and the best ways of demonstrating positive results of in-service programs. Furthermore, a growing body of literature and emphasis in the field (Fingeret and Cockley, 1992; Jones, 1991) suggests that learners need to play a more prominent role in determining and addressing their own staff development needs. In fact, Fingeret and Cockley (1992) note, "It is important to integrate a commitment to individual teacher growth and development with an understanding of the importance of community, program growth, collaborative work, and shared learning" (p. 21).

A strong in-service program generally includes elements of the following: a needs assessment process, matching the needs with the audience, program design, program implementation, evaluation, and follow-up. Within each aspect of this plan is the need to maximize the integration of the needs of the teacher and student at all times.

Determining Needs

The consensus of adult education practitioners is that significant learning will take place when topics discussed address problems for the learner. "The learning experience should develop from the level of participants' understanding, background and experience, and it should be based on the needs and interests that they themselves feel or that they can be assisted to recognize" (Rosenblum, 1985, p. 18).

In-service education is likely to be perceived as everyone's responsibility while it is often, in fact, nobody's assigned responsibility. Coordination has tended to be informal or nonexistent. Knox (1980) found that topics for teacher staff development activities have tended to be based on program planners' general (or perceived) familiarity with the needs of workshop participants rather than on formal needs assessments.

Systematic needs assessments are essential to planning in-service programs. Rubin and Hansen (1980) suggest that these needs should be analyzed and translated into goals or desired training outcomes and prioritized to consider present as well as future needs. In a recent study of adult basic education/English as a second language (ABE/ESL) teacher training approaches (Pelavin and Associates, 1991), a variety of needs assessment processes were identified. It was found that a majority of needs assessments at the state and regional levels were done by statewide agencies. Furthermore, administrators tended to make topic decisions in the majority of cases.

Determining needs is difficult. In more traditional models of staff development, a top-down training plan is used, in which the administration determines the needs of the staff and plans staff development activities accordingly. Furthermore, the "expert" presenter is frequently enlisted with the prerequisite skills matched to address the identified needs.

Recent views of staff development seek to involve participants more actively in determining their own needs. This approach involves helping learners identify background experiences and establish their relevance to new learning. Staff development should be consistent with this thinking. "Teachers' existing knowledge should be understood as a resource that supports continued learning, and . . . there should be a clear relationship between the kind of learning opportunities provided for teachers and the way in which we hope those teachers will work with their students" (Fingeret and Cockley, 1992, p. 2).

A Virginia study of staff development concluded, "The extent to which any one activity is useful depends upon the teacher's characteristics and how the teacher connects it to his or her situation and ways of learning" (Fingeret and Cockley, 1992, p. 16).

Defining the Audience and Matching Needs

Frequently, to become an adult education instructor, minimal credentials—often only an advanced degree or expertise in a specialty area—are required to teach. English as a second language (ESL), adult basic education (ABE), and general educational development (GED) programs often attract teachers who have a variety of experiences; those with extensive school teaching experience may be employed along with those who have minimal teaching experience but extensive content knowledge (as in reading or foreign language), or individuals may be employed with extensive years of adult education experience. Activities such as small-group work that provide experienced staff with an opportunity to share information with less experienced staff offer maximum flexibility to accommodate diverse interests and experiences. These activities need to be structured to provide maximum participation of all instructors.

The diverse needs of adult education instructors combined with the largely part-time nature of the field requires an efficient design and a well-matched delivery system. Activities need to be scheduled when the majority of staff are free, often evenings or Saturdays. Similarly, training activities are often best developed as half-day sessions to accommodate staff availability.

Designing and Implementing the Program

Identifying Clear Objectives. Based on needs assessment findings, a clear direction for training is essential. It is generally agreed that the determination of objectives for a program is the next step in the staff development activity planning process. Rosenblum (1985) states, "Objectives help in framing the learning activity into a logical sequence, in selecting resources and techniques, and in determining topics to be included or emphasized" (p. 18).

Cooper and Jones (1984), citing Stubblefield, suggest two ways of matching participant expectations with preidentified needs. The instructor may invite participants to talk about what they expect to get out of their learning experience and how they expect to go about it. Or an instructor may simply tell participants what they will be expected to do and the intended benefits. Cooper and Jones suggest that a combination of these two approaches may achieve the maximum benefit.

In-Service Training. Jones (1991), in his research of staff development of elementary and secondary education content areas, found remarkable similarities to adult education interest areas. The most common emerging areas of elementary and secondary education staff development interest included higher-order thinking skills, learning styles, models of teaching, classroom interaction patterns, computer applications, and writing skills.

Nunes and Halloran (1991) identify eight teachable skills and competencies constituting successful performance of ABE instruction: knowledge of the adult learner, personal qualities, knowledge of the field, knowledge of teaching techniques, creativity, communication and interpersonal skills, professionalism, and management organization. The Teaching Improvement Process (TIP) created by the Center for Adult Education at San Francisco State University notes six categories of teaching skills necessary for excellence in adult education instruction: overall organization of the learning activity, life skills competency application, monitoring student performance, teaching to a variety of student learning styles, appropriateness of materials, and classroom grouping strategies (Pelavin and Associates, 1991).

Preservice. Training before employment, or preservice, is rare in the field of adult education. With few bachelor's degree programs, varied local and state teacher requirements, high teacher turnover, the need to fill part-time positions quickly, and difficulty in locating potential instructors, preservice staff development activities are extremely difficult to organize and implement. The need for preservice exists; however, the mechanism and ability to capture this audience present special problems.

In a recent Preservice Institute, sponsored by the Adult Learning Resource Center (Des Plaines, Illinois), individuals from a variety of teaching assignments and other professions participated in a four-day preservice staff development activity. Participants, none of whom was currently in the field, were attracted through local county educational service regions, workplace announcements, and local elementary and secondary substitute teacher lists. Participants primarily registered because they wanted to know more about the field; some were considering adult education for employment (Adult Learning Resource Center, 1992). This Preservice Institute included survey topics on the adult learner, cross-cultural awareness, goal setting, and monitoring instruction. Other skill areas included mathematics instructional methodology, adult reading techniques, ESL methods, and assessment.

In local programs, preservice is infrequent and difficult to implement. This is largely because program orientation needs are the primary focus. These sessions often address program logistics, registration and enrollment forms, attendance procedures, and employment requirements, but leave little opportunity to discuss instructional content and methods.

Follow-up. Frequently, there is little long-term planning for in-service programs. One-shot training sessions may do well in presenting an overview or introducing a concept, but "if the purpose of an inservice is to integrate learning into an existing curriculum (or staff development plan) then more in-depth training as well as appropriate follow-up will be required" (Cooper and Jones, 1984, p. 42). In fact, in the study by Pelavin and Associates (1991) surveying state and regional adult education staff development, it was found that a majority of activities were single-session activities, while follow-up sessions were seldom used.

Matching Content with Needs

Identifying Presenters. Content knowledge and training methodology are equally important to consider when selecting a presenter for a staff development activity. The background knowledge of the presenter combined with strong "walk your adult talk" presentation skills will prove to be the most successful. An approach that combines new content information with strong facilitating skills that recognize the experiences of participants provides the best framework for addressing the potentially broad range of participant skills and needs.

Sometimes "going outside" for a presenter is not the best recourse. Local program contexts, politics, and needs may not be easily addressed by an outside "expert." Experienced local staff members frequently have the ability, interest, and personal resources to provide a quality staff development activity. Staff members at existing state and regional adult education resource centers and the emerging State Literacy Resource Centers provided under the National Literacy Act of 1991 are surely viable resources for adult education staff development activities. However, discretion is advisable if local staff members may be capable of providing a staff development activity alone.

Additional Resources. The use of video to demonstrate new techniques and components of the adult classroom is an excellent, effective manner to present a variety of information. Video is a consistent, effective way to present teaching techniques. It provides realistic contexts and classrooms with "real" students; it also frequently captures classroom variables often missing from a secondhand presentation.

Although using video is not a new concept, participants in several recent Adult Learning Resource Center activities have commented that the use of video has given them a better understanding of adult classrooms and methods of presenting content (Adult Learning Resource Center, 1992).

Another resource supplementing staff development activities is handouts to support and reinforce the content. Presenters frequently provide many more handouts than are actually needed or even useful in a presentation. Using only the most appropriate handouts and most relevant reference articles appears to be most effective. Given the largely part-time nature of the field, efficiency tends to be the best gauge for measuring the quantity of handouts and written supplementary materials.

Integrating Principles of Effective Staff Development into Training

Recent research on effective staff development training has revealed a variety of essential components, which are described in the following section.

Needs should be identified systematically. "The group most affected by the training should have a strong voice in identifying the needs on which these activities are based" (Pelavin and Associates, 1991, p. III-31). Others—including students, administrators, and employers—should be considered in the needs assessment process. (See the discussion of the issue of proficient staff for needs analyses in Chapter One and project need and problem statement in Chapter Three.)

Teacher-participants should be involved in planning and decision making. Ownership of the training event is a direct result of teacher involvement in the planning and development of an activity.

A positive climate for teacher growth and change should be maintained. Teacher growth and change are fostered in a climate in which "the administrator is viewed primarily as an instructional leader, and a climate that encourages experimentation and risk-taking" (Pelavin and Associates, 1991, p. III-34). In many adult education programs, the administrator has little time to develop or even maintain an instructional leadership role; and frequently, "lead instructors" assume curriculum and program leadership. To obtain and maintain this positive environment for growth, teachers need support, release time, and recognition for their efforts to implement new ideas.

An effective program reflects up-to-date knowledge and the underlying goals of the program. Current knowledge of the field is essential in an effective model. For example, if a program places emphasis on a specific instructional philosophy such as whole language, the selected training should support these efforts.

An effective staff development program should reflect continuity. This is demonstrated through follow-up efforts and transfer to classroom settings.

In the Pelavin and Associates study (1992), six principles were identified as essential organizing components. These include theory, demonstration, practice, structured feedback, application, and reflection opportunities.

Theory. Collins (1981) states that in-service programs characterized by a balance between theory and practice have the most overall impact and the greatest appeal to participants. The theory provides the overall structure and validity for the training activity.

Demonstration. Demonstration provides a first-hand presentation of a technique through either video or a presentation by a trainer.

Practice. Participants have the opportunity to practice a technique or approach in the context of training, often with the support or guidance of a facilitator or session leader.

Structured feedback. The structured feedback approach allows participants to compare, analyze, and synthesize applications of techniques in a controlled environment.

Application. Participants have the opportunity to apply demonstrated and practiced techniques in a new situation.

Reflection. Participants are given a variety of opportunities to reflect on new instructional approaches and their applications. Furthermore, participants become conscious of the theories and assumptions that underlie and guide these approaches.

Developing and Implementing an Evaluation Plan

Evaluations serve to assess a training activity or, more importantly, to provide direction for future training plans. Evaluations can use numerical indicators or participant surveys, each of which are most commonly used following a staff development activity.

If evaluations use only numerical ratings, they may overlook essential information that open-ended questions may elicit. Questions could be phrased as follows: What did you find most effective? What part would you change? One problem I solved today was _____. The questions provide a focus for the participant's response and often substantive information for future training design.

Baden (1982, p. 37) suggested five questions that might best guide the desired results of an in-service evaluation: "Was the content of the in-service activity informative and useful to the participants? Was the presenter of the in-service activity effective? Did the participants in the in-service activity exhibit the behavior change defined by the objectives? Did the participants' behavior in their classrooms change as a result of the in-service activity after a period of time? Did the students of the participants change as a result of teachers' altered behavior?"

Each of these questions must be tied to the original needs assessment findings and the identified objectives and session goals. Although it is helpful to get initial session feedback, immediate responses may often be influenced by the "halo" effect and may fall short of revealing the actual effectiveness of training. Follow-up surveys and evaluations done six weeks or a few months after an activity can provide information on longer-term application and training effectiveness.

The Adult Learning Resource Center began using a postcard follow-up evaluation of its regional activities in early 1992. Participants are sent a short self-addressed postcard evaluation form two months following a selected training activity. Participants are asked to respond to questions about the content of the workshop, the application of techniques to their teaching situation, any impediments to this implementation, and recommendations for future training. This information has been helpful in redesigning many training activities as well as assessing long-term training impact.

The largest role of evaluation is not in the preservice or in-service plan itself but in the long-term application of its content to the instructional plan.

Johnson (1980) suggests there should be a continuum in preservice and in-service education that reflects competencies at each stage of teacher development. These competencies obviously affect the application of skills and the actual desired teacher performance in the classroom. (See the discussion of assessment of project evaluation in Chapter Three, collection of evaluation data in Chapter Seven, and preparation for evaluation in Chapter Nine.)

Involving the Participant Actively

An important aspect of any staff development program and one that is increasingly becoming the dominant force in adult education staff development training is the learner's active participation in his or her own educational process. Knowles (1975) recognizes the need for this vital learner role. He states, "This perspective is found in the work of humanistic educators who argue that education should aim at helping the learner to develop skills of inquiry that enable the individual (with or without the help of others) to take the initiative in a self-directed learning process. Learners should be able to assess their own learning needs and objectives, identify human and material resources, and develop, implement, and evaluate appropriate learning strategies" (p. 21). (See the discussion of participatory research in Chapter Two and learning contracts in Chapter Nine.)

Emerging approaches to adult staff development with more active participation of the learner or participant include action research, inquiry-based research, and self-study. Each recognizes the basic principle that adults can best determine their needs and the necessary means to address them.

The Adult Learning Resource Center has initiated a variety of provider groups in recent years. These groups are organized around interest areas such as family literacy, GED, Spanish literacy, or work force literacy. Within this provider framework are opportunities to discuss participant-determined topics. Scheduled on a bimonthly or quarterly basis, these meetings address a wide range of topics related to provider group member interest areas. No single "expert" is used with these groups unless specifically requested as a resource. Each group prepares activities and identifies resources for the regular meetings, and an ongoing needs assessment process creates topics for subsequent meetings.

In another participant-centered form of staff development, action research, teachers' experience and knowledge are used and provide the base for continuing inquiry, learning, and actions. This model of staff development is also referred to as the inquiry-based model. Lytle and Cochran-Smith (1990) describe it as a "systematic, intentional inquiry by teachers about their own school and classroom work" (p. 84).

When viewed as inquiry-based action, staff development depends less on expert workshops and more on teacher-led activities. Lieberman and Miller

(1991) state, "These activities can include study groups, curriculum writing, action research, peer observation, case conferences, program evaluation, practice of new techniques, teacher centers, and participation in outside events and organizations" (p. 92).

In a Virginia staff development study (Fingeret and Cockley, 1992), teachers commented they "would like the opportunity to learn from other teachers in a more formalized manner" (p. 13). Furthermore, the Virginia study proposed a model of staff development in which teacher's questions in relation to practice drive learning rather than experts' advice. The teacher rather than the training becomes the center of the learning process.

Action research also lends itself well to ongoing monitoring. The instructor acting as researcher, reflecting on methods being used, and modifying them for maximum instructional benefit creates an expanded role for evaluation. The key is using this data on an ongoing basis to improve instruction.

In the Action Research Professional Development Program, a systematic structure is added to the teacher's research plan (Mezirow, 1992). In monitoring sheets that accompany the program, teachers are asked to respond to specific questions when summarizing their own action research, including these: How did you use the practice? What were the results? What is your interpretation of the results? These questions afford the teacher-participant an important opportunity to reflect on the technique used and record a response.

Conclusion

A balance between content-driven staff development activities led by outside specialists and learner-centered designs is essential. The varied nature of adult education employment suggests that a core of basic adult education teaching skills is needed. Because of the diverse experiences of instructors and the varied requirements for teaching adults, instructors need a well-focused, efficient staff development plan. The plan must be flexible and must recognize individual experiences while it accommodates long-term professional growth.

The Virginia Staff Development Study (Fingeret and Cockley, 1992) recognized these adult education staff development variables and provided recommendations for a model staff development program. The study concluded that the following elements are part of an effective staff development plan:

Teachers are helped to use what they know to continue learning.
Activities, attitudes, structure, and values support building a community of teachers as well as a community of teachers and learners.
There is a focus on the interrelatedness of all aspects of adult education programs.
Staff development is viewed as a continuing process involving administrators as well as teachers.

References

Adult Learning Resource Center. Preservice Institute Evaluation Data. Des Plaines, Ill.: Adult Learning Resource Center, Summer 1992.

Baden, D. J. "A User's Guide to the Evaluation of Staff Development." In F. J. McDonald, W. J. Rapham, and D. J. Baden, Assessing the Impact of Staff Development Programs. Syracuse, N.Y.: National Council of States on Inservice Education, 1982.

Collins, J. F. "The State of the Art in Inservice Education and Staff Development in State Departments of Education and the Federal Department of Education." Journal of Research and Development in Education, 1981, 15, 13–19.

Cooper, C. M., and Jones, E. V. "The State of the Art in Inservice Education: A Review of the Literature." Fairfax, Va.: Division of Continuing Education, George Mason University, 1984.

Fingeret, H. A., and Cockley, S. Teachers Learning: An Evaluation of ABE Staff Development in Virginia. Dayton: Virginia Adult Educator's Network, 1992.

Johnson, M. Inservice Education: Priorities for the 80's. Syracuse, N.Y.: National Council of State on Inservice Education, 1980.

Jones, E. V. What Adult Basic Education Staff Development Can Learn from K–12 Staff Development. Fairfax, Va.: Division of Continuing Education, George Mason University, 1991.

Knowles, M. S. Self-Directed Learning. Chicago: Association Press, Follett, 1975.

Knox, A. B. "Continuing Professional Education for School Teachers and Administrators." In J. C. Fever (ed.), Coordinating College of Education Inservice Programs. Proceedings of the First National Conference of College of Education Inservice Coordinators. Madison: University of Wisconsin, 1980.

Knox, A. B. "Educational Leadership and Program Administration." In J. M. Peters, P. Jarvis, and Associates, Adult Education: Evolution and Achievements in a Developing Field of Study. San Francisco: Jossey-Bass, 1991.

Lieberman, A., and Miller, L. "Revisiting the Social Realities of Teaching." In A. Lieberman and L. Miller (eds.), Staff Development for Education in the 90's: New Demands, New Realities, New Perspectives. (2nd ed.) New York: Teachers College Press, 1991.

Lytle, S., and Cochran-Smith, M. "Teacher Research: A Working Typology." Teachers College Record, 1990, 92 (1), 83–103.

Mezirow, J. "Action Research Professional Development Program." New York: New York Institute for Adult Development, 1992.

Nunes, S. H., and Halloran, T. F. "Elements for a Training Design: Assessment of Competencies for Effective ABE Instructors." Tallahassee: Florida State Department of Education, 1987.

Pelavin and Associates, Inc., San Francisco State University, and the Adult Learning Resource Center. "Study of ABE/ESL Instructor Training Approaches State of the Practice Report." Office of Vocational and Adult Education, U.S. Department of Education, 1991.

Pelavin and Associates, Inc., San Francisco State University, and the Adult Learning Resource Center. "Study of ABE/ESL Instruction Training Approaches Phase I Technical Report." Office of Vocational and Adult Education, U.S. Department of Education, 1992.

Rosenblum, S. H., (ed.). Involving Adults in the Educational Process. New Directions for Continuing Education, no. 26. San Francisco: Jossey-Bass, 1985.

Rubin, L., and Hansen, J. L. "Assessing Needs and Prioritizing Goals." In W. R. Houston and R. Pankratz (eds.), Staff Development and Educational Change. Reston, Va.: Association of Teacher Educators, 1980.

Strother, G. B., and Klus, J. P. Administration of Continuing Education. Belmont, Calif.: Wadsworth, 1982.

DENNIS TERDY is director of the Adult Learning Resource Center (ALRC) in Des Plaines, Illinois. The ALRC and Pelavin Associates, San Francisco State University, recently completed a two-year study funded by the U.S. Department of Education.

Technology trends can be identified to improve the efficiency of adult education administration. Five management functions and three technology groups are the focus of this chapter.

Improving Administrative Efficiency Through Technology

Dennis R. Porter

The U.S. work force continues to change (Johnson and Packer, 1987). Three demographic variables symbolize and describe the labor changes: gender, ethnicity, and age. The value of knowledge used in manufacturing and service industries defines our competitiveness in the global economy (Reich, 1991; Sakaiya, 1991). Smart manufacturing is seen as central to our long-term economic interests.

Lifelong learning and retraining are no longer slogans. Knowledge and information are the keys to productivity. Administrators of adult education programs, from basic education to continuing professional education, will be seriously challenged to meet these new demands. The demands may induce changes in the organizational cultures administrators have helped construct and that have in turn influenced their administrative views.

How do desktop technologies affect the adult education administrator? They strongly imply decentralized authority, oversight, and communications along with increased effectiveness and efficiency. This chapter examines five management functions and suggests communications and software applications to improve the adult education administrator's efficiency and effectiveness. The instructor's access to learning enrichment tools is linked to the administrator's oversight responsibilities. The chapter concludes that appropriate technologies will enhance service delivery, and the implications of failing to consider technologies and the resultant competitive disadvantage to the administrator are raised.

Impacts of Technology

Telecommunications and desktop computer technologies are refining the way Americans access and use information and knowledge. These new technologies affect how and what we learn. Three examples indicate implications for the adult education administrator:

Virtual Classroom™. The notion of the "virtual classroom" is being promoted, in which learning is no longer classroom based, but primarily on-line (electronic) and driven by learner-instruction interactions, with only occasional meetings. The originators of the concept conceived of a "group communication workspace and facilities connected in software" (Hiltz, 1990, pp. 59–65). These interactions are coordinated through electronic bulletin board or remote electronic mail (e-mail) and file transfer capabilities. One-to-one electronic communications, one-to-many, and many-to-many communications are possible. Collaborative learning is stressed, with active participation and interactions between instructors and learners. It can occur in a local setting or in a remote setting in which most communications occur via computer ("A College Degree . . . ," 1992, p. 83).

In addition to playing the traditional role of teacher, the teacher can be a mentor and guide (Merriam and Cunningham, 1990; Houle, 1992). In this model students can become teachers. Assignments and projects are conducted individually and in small groups. Some group activities can be based on simulated problem solving.

What is the administrator's role in examining this model? It may be to define the electronic infrastructure to permit more flexible learning. New procedures and interactions are required. An organizational climate that encourages this experimentation is essential. Testing and evaluation are needed to see when and how the concept flourishes. New resources may be necessary to underwrite the communications and user training. Different instructional skills may be required. These considerations affect the administrator's planning, organizing, staffing, and evaluation responsibilities.

Electronic document transfer. Currently, computer applications software determines the nature of the desktop publishing document. For example, word processors all perform differently. Formatting and display features (type fonts, size, and other graphical features) are often garbled when information from one word processor is exchanged with another. To date the same word processor or minimal formatting is required to facilitate file exchange.

Portable document formats will soon be available that will make the document the software core, not the application. The promise is that users can transfer digital (electronic) documents between Macintosh, DOS, Windows, and UNIX operating environments without a "significant loss of fonts or formatting" ("Adobe's Acrobat . . . ," 1992; "Does Adobe Have a Paper Cutter?" 1992). This is one major step in the increased use of electronic documents. Text search and optical character reader (scanning) capabilities will also be added.

This technology will enable professional personnel using their favorite word processors and support personnel using different desktop publishing software to exchange documents without formatting distortion. For example, I wrote this chapter using Microsoft Word for Windows. The editor used WordPerfect software to prepare the final manuscript. The conversion from one software to another was imperfect and required document reformatting, but in the future this problem will be eliminated. It will mark the beginning of electronic document libraries that are easy to use and share. This may increase the responsibility of the instructor to produce his or her own documents but will also enable him or her to assemble the documents, add other features like text search, and begin to build document libraries. Over time the addition of graphical, audio, or video features to these documents will lead to the often touted but still emerging multimedia technologies.

Distributed information. This type of management information storage and transfer implies that digital data are developed and maintained at various places but can be readily accessed by other users. Distributed information can take several forms; for example, it might be centralized, with ready access for desktop users. Current examples of mainframe and minicomputer management information systems (MISs) are numerous. Users can access pertinent information from the large computer at their desktop computers using simple software tools such as natural language queries that can be used occasionally without requiring substantial learning.

Distributed information may also take the form of digital information that is remotely accessible on local area networks (LANs) and wide area networks (WANs). This emerging technology makes information available (subject to authorization) from different storage locations.

The terminology currently used is client-server technology, in which substantial information is stored on a networked server computer that also operates the networking software. Single locations (nodes) on the network are desktop computers that perform various functions but also share information with the server and other locations as needed.

Both the LAN and the WAN are generic examples and cover a wide range of changes in software, communications, and hardware configurations. One administrative implication is that hardware purchase and maintenance and software development costs can be reduced. Another implication is that more information should be directly accessible to appropriate instructional staff, support staff, and administrators. Such access to information may change roles, responsibilities, and organizational hierarchies. It will promote computer-based information sharing, electronic mail, group scheduling, and group document development and will require less face-to-face communication for routine functions. (See the discussion of communications systems revisited in Chapter Five.)

Management Functions

Facilitating access to information and knowledge is a goal of the adult education administrator. Management is an integrating process. It involves decision making under conditions of uncertainty, communicating imperfect information in multiple channels, and engaging in endless rounds of planning, acting, and evaluating (Gross, 1968). (See the discussion of managing multiple grants in Chapter Three, the adult educator as manager of groups in Chapter Five, and management roles in Chapter Ten.)

There are five key adult education management functions (Porter, 1987) that form the basis for adult education administration:

Planning (forecasting, determining direction, action planning, and allocating resources)

Directing, facilitating, and empowering personnel (problem analysis, decision making, and communications)

Organizing work to meet desired results (structuring work, establishing and maintaining relationships, and delegating)

Staffing (selecting, training, and developing personnel)

Evaluating (determining standards, measuring and evaluating, and enhancing performance)

Each function can be refined and enhanced through appropriate technologies. The next section outlines examples to improve group and individual productivity.

Technology Applications

Three sets of technology applications are of particular interest to the administrator.

Computer-based communications. This includes the transfer of digital information among users and communicators. The focus is on electronic mail, digital file transmission, and computer networking.

California has a statewide adult education communications system that permits electronic mail (e-mail), along with file transfer, among any of its users. The system allows the writer to send messages or computer files to a mainframe computer to be retrieved at the convenience of the designated recipient or recipients. Group messages can be sent. In addition, a special adult education forum includes these components: adult education legislation, state department of education information, reference materials, lesson plans, course outlines, current articles, educational grants, public domain software, demonstration software, master calendar, want ads, and roundtable for special chats and work groups.

This system is managed under a grant from the state by the Hacienda La Puente School District. It uses a commercial vendor for the system and maintains its own forum with the above features. The key to the system is ease of use. Each major feature is given a designated icon (a graphical symbol) that can be accessed using a mouse or pointing device. A Macintosh computer or a personal computer using Windows is required. Users outside California can access the system if they obtain permission.

A long-term trend is the creation of a supercommunications network. Internet, the world's largest computer network, began as a method to link U.S. military and other researchers and is evolving into a tool for the occasional user and amateur as well as the sophisticated user. As a network of networks, it ties together a wide range of data bases, forums for communicating about myriad topics, and methods for transferring e-mail and files among users (Krol, 1992). In all likelihood Internet will form the electronic communications superhighway discussed as part of the current national political agenda.

Management information system (MIS) technology. The value of routine access to management information cannot be overstated. Data base technologies greatly facilitate this access. The trend in large organizations is toward moving these systems to smaller computers and using newer, faster desktop software in smaller administrative units. Often there is a distinction between program information about the learner and course and core management information—accounting, personnel administration, and facilities management.

The information in an MIS can range from student records, class rosters, and course listings, to mailing lists, equipment inventories, personnel records, and accounting systems. Software that links several of these information types is usually relational, that is, it can build information relations between data files such as student records, class rosters, and class listings.

Desktop applications software. This software includes the full range of software tools available to support administration. Examples include word processors, spreadsheets, accounting software, graphics and design tools, data base software, project management software, desktop publishing, statistical analysis software, communications software, presentation software, programming languages, software system utilities, multimedia tools (audio and video hardware and software), computer-assisted design, and personal and group scheduling.

There are overlaps among the examples just given. Some are available in special software versions developed for the adult educator. They are also available as applications software to be developed by the user.

The relative value of a software vendor or system integrator's products is a matter of endless debate. The selection is a function of the computer operating system or operating environment, and the objectives, human and fiscal resources, and administrator choice ("The Administration Problem," 1992). Experience indicates that these applications software packages will be significantly upgraded every eighteen to twenty-four months. Specially developed software is usually upgraded on a licensing basis.

Table 7.1 cross-references some of these software tools with the five management functions. The communications examples are a combination of hardware and software.

Important administration roles are defining how the applied technologies support the management functions and determining the necessary improvements. Any steps taken to improve computer-based communications should enhance administration if they are simple and understandable. For all the technologies listed, current emphasis is on making the user's interaction with the software simple, straightforward, and intuitive.

Planning activities are best improved by developing and maintaining information on who the learners are, what their needs and interests are, and likely changes in particular learning markets. Good planning requires balancing the service objectives with the user characteristics, the available resources, and the organizational conditions and structure (Porter, 1989), necessitating historical information on learners and access to research information about targeted learners.

Both administrators and instructional personnel should have access to these data. The ability to access and perform analyses of these data rapidly is very important. This enables administrators to control MIS functions (rather than simply being recipients of information maintained outside the adult education realm). Information on how other learning providers address the same programs or courses should be maintained.

The directing, facilitating, and empowering function is best supported by having computer-based communications among all personnel. The ideal form depends on the nature and size of the organization. For example, if the adult education mission is integrated into a larger learning system, the electronic communications will likely serve all users. The communications system will likely serve only the adult education personnel if the provider is a single-purpose adult education system or if it functions in a decentralized system where adult education essentially stands alone.

Access to MIS data and computer-based tools is important. The very clear trend is to move MIS and administration and course development software tools to the desktop, where staff members will have direct access to them. The same applies to research and information data bases that can support instruction.

Increased efficiencies in the work organization function come from electronic communications and ready access to MIS data and desktop software for carrying out tasks. An important administrative responsibility is to help create an environment in which these technologies are accepted. Project management software that plots tasks, time lines, and budgets is a very useful tool for regular and occasional activities and projects.

The staffing function can also be improved by communications technologies and training in the use of and access to software tools. A simple example is on-line access to information on one's own vacation and sick time. Another

**Table 7.1. Matrix of Administrative Technologies
and Management Functions**

Management Functions/ Technologies and Communications Technology	Management Information System Technology	Desktop Applications Software
Planning		
Electronic access to learner database statistics	Strategic planning data—learner profiles, pre-post test scores, demographic characteristics, database of users	Project planning and management software
Access to electronic research databases such as ERIC, Dialog, CompuServe, Dow Jones News/Retrieval, OTAN, Internet	Expert system software monitoring significant trends	Spreadsheet and other simple forms of program budgeting
		Mapping software to display key data
		Computer assisted design
		Personal information managers
Directing, facilitating, and empowering personnel		
Local area network (LAN)—reporting	Query access to program information	Groupware and file sharing tools
Electronic mail	Policy of information sharing and access	Budget and project management information scheduling
On-line file sharing	Document libraries—trend toward instructional courseware	Individual and group sheduling
Organizing work		
Local area network (LAN)—reporting	Program performance and demographic data	Project planning software
Electronic mail	Attendance accounting software	Project budgeting software
On-line appointment and group calendar	Access to research databases	Grant and other proposal development—word processing, desktop publishing, statistical tools
On-line access to electronic databases	Queries and reports from administrative and program databases	Attendance scanning tools
Staffing		
On-line access to professional development budgets and resources	Personnel policies and procedures on-line	Group development activities
	Budgets for human resource development	Project budgeting software
Evaluating		
Local area network (LAN)—reporting	Access to learner performance and learner satisfaction data	Statistical analysis packages
Electronic mail	Encouragement of continued product evaluation and innovation based on evaluation data	Project accounting
		Project planning software
		Mapping software to display key data

example is the electronic group scheduling of vacation and out-of-the-office time so an administrator can have instant access to the information.

The evaluation function is easy to overlook. Administrators and instructional personnel alike are often convinced that they know what works and why. They may prefer anecdotal and practical experience to more systematic information. This predilection should be seriously resisted. One way is to have evaluation information collected systematically and made available in summary form to the administrator. Learner satisfaction and suggestions are data that should be routinely collected and analyzed. (See the discussion of the assessment of project evaluation in Chapter Three, the role of evaluation in staff development in Chapter Six, and the preparation for evaluation in Chapter Nine.)

Because evaluation and planning are strategically linked, the data important for one function are important for the other. A good MIS is key to the function. Demographic and other descriptive information on the current, past, and probable learner is essential. Information on learner satisfaction and recommendations are important. One approach is to be certain that current and objective management information is available on the organization's weaknesses, opportunities, threats, and strengths.

The current emphasis on ease of use strongly suggests that software that takes advantage of the graphical user interface be used. This interface is also referred to as windows, because options and functions are usually displayed in a series of on-screen boxes or windows. A distinguishing feature is the use of icons and symbols to denote choices. The four most prevalent windows operating environments are the Macintosh, Windows for DOS, OS/2 (the new IBM operating system), and X-windows for UNIX computers.

It is now feasible to embed voice messages in shared software. These messages are expected to clarify or explain particular points. The use of voice commands with desktop software will begin to appear in the next several years. The software will recognize certain voice commands that were formally carried out with keystrokes or mouse clicks. Handwriting recognition capabilities will soon be common with some desktop and hand-held computers. These changes will redefine ease of use again.

A simple example of how this technology may work in the future is the use of hand-held computers with check boxes or other input systems to maintain class attendance information on a weekly basis. Attendance by day can be checked. The data can be easily transferred from the hand-held device to the computer that maintains these data. These devices will soon be cost-effective because they save instructors recording time and reduce staff input and processing time. The data should be more accurate than with current manual and "bubble" approaches.

Implications

These technologies make information more directly and readily available. Their informed use can produce increased access to administrative data, improved information sharing, decentralized information management and decision making, curricular changes and enhancements, and remote access to research information. None of these changes in themselves has a value. The value added is determined by how the change is used to meet adult education objectives.

Administrative technologies may reduce the need for middle- and senior-level managers and support staff. Instructional personnel will have more access to computer-based production tools and will require less support, which could have profound effects on administrative arrangements. A tension between the way things are and more reliance on technology is probable.

Personnel functions are likely to change as the administrative technologies are introduced and mature. The implications vary according to the organization and the number of full-time equivalent staff; however, it is clear that fewer persons will be required to carry out the same tasks. This will be true in all organizations as routine tasks become increasingly automated.

Thurow (1992, p. 175) provides a forceful example of one effect. In discussing the use of word processors and why they have not led to the predicted gains in productivity, he observes that efficient office automation requires major changes in office sociology. "The efficient way to use word processors is to eliminate secretaries or clerks and to require managers to type their own memos and call up their own files. But a personal secretary is an office badge of prestige and power. No one wants to give up that badge."

Organizing for Changing Technology

Introducing administrative technology requires user participation in the planning and implementation. Sufficient time should be allowed to orient and train the users. Initial utilization should be more instructive than organizational. How the applications are used will change with more experience.

It is important to standardize key aspects of shared software or shared files. Using templates or scripts to automate the information will save significant time, especially when inputting, editing, and reformatting information. Word processing and desktop publishing software allow the user to create templates or style sheets to automate key formatting activities. Organizational styles for reports, memos, letters, and other documents can be defined by using templates that pick the font size and style, paragraph parameters, borders, tabs, headline format, and so forth.

Increasingly, it is possible to link documents or objects within documents to other documents. For example, a spreadsheet program that maintains monthly budget information can be dynamically linked to a written monthly report and associated graphs that will change with new monthly data. The core report form will be constant, but the data will change monthly. If new comments, analyses, or additions are required, they can be added to the report. This saves substantial time and avoids data entry mistakes. More attention should be paid, however, to creating the original document formats.

These same linking features are now appearing in data base and other applications software. For example, an administrator can conceivably link information from an accounting data base to a project management program, to a summary spreadsheet report complete with graphic displays of resource allocations, to an administrative report incorporating the graphs. These dynamic data will change as information in the accounting data base are added.

Policy Issues

The policy issues associated with improving administrative efficiencies through technology include software and communications continuity and comparability with other organizational units, priority setting, and roles and responsibilities. The policy solutions will vary substantially depending on location, organizational culture, and leadership. New personnel skills will be required. Except in large organizations, specialist personnel, for the most part, should not be required. (See also the discussion of resource issues in Chapter One and "at home" issues in Chapter Two.)

Benefits and Costs

In my experience, the classical examination of benefits and costs often does not apply when discussing administrative technology. Rather, there are opportunity costs that are part benefit and part cost. Technology allows the administrator to be free from certain tasks, make certain tasks more efficient, or improve on the tasks. These enhancements offer opportunities to pursue other activities. Measuring the utility of pursuing these new activities or enhanced opportunities is the crux of the analysis. Often there are not personnel changes but rather changes in personnel functions. An objective is to automate routine tasks when feasible.

Analyses based on the "cost of quality" are becoming increasingly popular. The premise is that qualitative and quantitative improvements in production have costs associated with them. However, there are often greater costs associated with poor quality. Examining costs of making and not making technology improvements can be a starting point in determining the utility of new administrative technologies.

Conclusion

Directed adult learning has never been centered entirely in the classroom. However, communications and computer technologies will continue the distribution of learning to suit the "any time, any place, any pace" paradigm. Adult and continuing education will continue to redefine modes of instruction via electronic communications, telecommunications, learning labs, mobile study groups, and multimedia libraries. Access to on-line research tools will improve and become more a part of the learning environment.

Will the administrator lead and encourage these changes? Will he or she resist them because they do not conform with an administrative model? It is suggested that the adult instructor's role is more and more frequently that of mentor and guide. The same can be said of the administrator. There is more emphasis on facilitation and empowerment of staff. Using the technologies discussed here will strengthen this trend.

Access to information is an attribute of administrative and professional power. Ready access to management information and to software tools for enriching instruction will be major themes in effective adult education administration. The administrator who supports access to and use of information and knowledge development tools will be the winner. There is little doubt that such an administrator will also change administrative arrangements.

Like many changes, introducing administrative technologies should be partially planned and based partially on creative muddling. The planning aspect comes from collective evaluation, planning, implementing, and refining the selection and use of these technologies. The muddling comes from the willingness to make mistakes, examine and learn from them, and make adjustments.

References

"The Administration Problem: New Software Programs Can Beat the Recordkeeping Blues." *Adult Learning*, 1992, *1* (4), 29–30.

"Adobe's Acrobat Promises Move to Paperless Office." *InfoWorld*, Nov. 23, 1992, p. 3.

"A College Degree—Via Your PC and VCR." *Business Week*, Dec. 1992, p. 116, E-2.

"Does Adobe Have a Paper Cutter?" *Business Week*, Nov. 16, 1992, p. 83.

Gross, B. *Organizations and Their Managing*. New York: Free Press, 1968.

Hiltz, S. R. "Collaborative Learning: The Virtual Classroom Approach," *Technological Horizons in Education (THE) Journal*, 1990, *17* (10), 59–65.

Houle, C. O. *The Literature of Adult Education: A Bibliographic Essay*. San Francisco: Jossey-Bass, 1992.

Johnson, W., and Packer, A. *Workforce 2000*. Indianapolis, Ind.: Hudson Institute, 1987.

Krol, E. *The Whole Internet*. Sebastopol, Calif.: O'Reilly and Associates, 1992.

Merriam, S. B., and Cunningham, P. M. (eds.). *Handbook of Adult and Continuing Education*. San Francisco: Jossey-Bass, 1989.

Porter, D. *The Strategic Management of Public Service Organizations*. Berkeley, Calif.: Micro Methods, Inc., 1987.

Porter, D. *The Role of MIS in Monitoring and Evaluation*. Berkeley, Calif.: Micro Methods, Inc., 1989.

Reich, R. *The Work of Nations*. New York: Knopf, 1991.

Sakaiya, T. *The Knowledge–Value Revolution*. New York: Kodansha America, 1991.

Thurow, L. *Head to Head*. New York: Morrow, 1992.

DENNIS R. PORTER is president of Micro Methods, Inc., Berkeley, California. Micro Methods focuses on knowledge and information system development and the use of instructional technologies in adult education.

Important reasons are explained for preparing for a useful, feasible, ethical, and accurate adult education evaluation.

Preparing for an Adult Education Evaluation

Robert C. Mason

This chapter emphasizes the importance of properly preparing for an adult education evaluation. It also discusses defining and identifying evaluations in adult education, recognizing the importance of standards and criteria for an appropriate educational evaluation, involving stakeholders and consultative groups in evaluation, collecting and organizing evaluation information, conducting the self-evaluation, developing recommendations and commendations, managing the exit interview, and writing the evaluation report for action.

Evaluation of adult education programs may well be the key to success of the field in the future. Evaluation, if effectively conducted and appropriately applied, can help adult educators squeeze maximum value from shrinking resources and can help demonstrate the importance of adult continuing education to society and the institution, agency, or organization sponsoring adult education programs. Therefore, the challenges of and the opportunities presented by adult education evaluation are tremendous. But the risks are great also; for if the evaluation is not appropriately conducted or is weak, then both the field of adult education practice and the program being evaluated are jeopardized.

Defining and Identifying Purposes of Evaluation

The term *evaluation* is defined by many different authors, and most of them would concur that it refers to the process of determining the worth or value of a program, a project, or something. Scriven (1991) defines *evaluation* as follows: The key sense of the term *evaluation* refers to the process of determining the merit, worth, or value of something, or the product of that process. Terms used to refer to this process or part of it include appraise, analyze, assess, critique, examine, grade, inspect, judge, rate, rank, review, study, test. A longer list including a number of terms that are only used evaluatively in special contexts would also include accredit, adjudicate, allocate, apportion, appraise, appreciation, audit, and benchmark.

In summary, evaluation often distinguishes good programs from bad programs, and, as Scriven (1991) mentions, evaluation can help separate food from garbage. (See the discussion of the assessment of project evaluation in Chapter Three, the role of evaluation in staff development in Chapter Six, and the collection of evaluation data in Chapter Seven.)

Using the Joint Committee's Standards for an Educational Evaluation

Twelve professional organizations appointed a seventeen-member committee that developed standards of excellence for evaluations. Additional input was sought from hundreds of practicing evaluation professionals. Standards were published by the Joint Committee on Standards for Educational Evaluation (1981), and these standards have had a dramatic impact on the ways in which the practice of evaluation has developed and changed during the past fifteen years.

The four major standards developed to evaluate the evaluation were utility, feasibility, propriety, and accuracy. Thirty-one substandards are contained under each one of these major standards. It is suggested that anyone serious about evaluation should read the Joint Committee on Standards for Educational Evaluation's (1981) Standards for Evaluations of Educational Programs, Projects, and Materials.

Daniel Stufflebeam (1980, p. 90), who was chair of the committee, indicated that the committee specified the order of the standards.

> The standards that will be published essentially call for evaluations that have four features. These are utility, feasibility, propriety and accuracy. And I think it is interesting that the Joint Committee decided on that particular order. Their rationale is that an evaluation should not be done at all if there is no prospect for its being useful to some audience. Second, it should not be done if it is not feasible to conduct it in political terms, or practicality terms, or cost effectiveness terms. Third, they do not think it should be done if we cannot demonstrate that it will be conducted fairly and ethically. Finally, if we can demonstrate that an evaluation will have utility, will be feasible and will be proper in its conduct then they said we could turn to the difficult matters of the technical adequacy of the evaluation, and they have included an extensive set of standards in this area [emphasis in original].

During the early years of evaluation, the emphasis was on accuracy, standard deviation, and statistical methods. Many evaluation reports gathered dust on the shelves and were never applied or used. Today there is more emphasis on the usefulness of evaluations, thanks in part to the standards of evaluation created by the Joint Committee. The standards have been very useful in assessing evaluations.

Reviewing the Criteria and Indicators of Quality

Most evaluations include rating against predetermined standards, criteria, or indicators of quality. Indicators of quality may include the number of books in the library or the qualifications of teachers. Standards were developed many years ago, especially for regional accreditation associations that evaluate secondary and postsecondary educational programs. Indicators of quality and standards are often developed by stakeholders associated closely with a program. Sometimes open hearings are held around a state, a region, or a nation to determine which standards or indicators of quality are most important. In the field of adult education, indicators of quality may include such items as curriculum and instructional materials, job placement, counseling, general administration, staffing and professional development, environment and technology, student or academic support services and activities, collaboration with other agencies, and evaluation and follow-up. Generally, team members grade or rate the program in accordance with the standards or indicators of quality. Several items to rate may be listed under each indicator of quality.

Involving the Stakeholder, Consultative Group, or Steering Committee

In his book Practical Evaluation, Patton (1982) emphasizes involvement of stakeholders and consultative groups. This suggestion has been very helpful to the process of adult education program evaluation. Stakeholders are people who have a vested interest in the program: teachers, students, governing board members, employees of social agencies, administrators, support services staff, and various employers. A good sample of the various stakeholders should be interviewed to help determine the worth of a program. Students enrolled in the program or graduates of the program are a very valuable source of stakeholder involvement and should not be overlooked. (See the discussion of selection of group members in Chapter Five, higher education stakeholders in Chapter Nine, and the humanistic administrator in Chapter Ten.)

Many evaluations could easily have a problem with propriety concerns or conflict of interest. A consultative group or a steering committee can help address many concerns about the usefulness, feasibility, propriety, and accuracy of the evaluation. The stakeholders and consultative group should be involved early and often throughout the evaluation process. This is especially important if an administrator or teacher is evaluating his or her own program. Involvement of other stakeholders or a consultative group can alleviate the potential conflict of interest. Moreover, there is a greater possibility that the evaluation will be utilized after its completion if the major stakeholders are involved throughout the evaluation process. Sometimes the involvement of stakeholders and consultative groups will require additional time for the evaluator and staff, but the investment in this effort is worthwhile. Stufflebeam (1980) aptly indicates that there is no need to conduct the evaluation if it will not be useful to the stakeholders and audiences involved.

Collecting and Organizing Evaluation Information

Most professional evaluators will request relevant documents: follow-up studies, class schedules, curriculum materials, performance reports, attendance and enrollment reports, previous evaluation reports, staff development plans, and a record of collaboration with other agencies and programs. It is very important for the adult education administrator and staff to provide this information in a useful and timely manner. It is most helpful if the relevant information can be sent to all of the evaluators several days or weeks ahead of time so they can thoroughly review the documents and prepare appropriate questions. A checklist related to the indicators of quality is shown in Exhibit 8.1.

Exhibit 8.1. Checklist

Demographic analysis report Enrollment reports: present and past two fiscal years Organizational chart	Job descriptions Strategic plan Promotional material samples Recruitment materials				
1. The demographic analysis is used in program planning.	1	2	3	4	NA
2. Program strives to create full-time administrative and teaching positions.	1	2	3	4	NA
3. Integration and coordination with other programs and services are evident.	1	2	3	4	NA
4. Program has developed a strategic plan for adult education in the commuity.	1	2	3	4	NA
5. Staff develops and promotes program information to constituents.	1	2	3	4	NA
6. Adequate staffing is available.	1	2	3	4	NA
7. Program is effective at marketing its services to recruit potential students.	1	2	3	4	NA

Criteria: 1 = there is no evidence; 2 = needs improvement; 3 = satisfactory; 4 = exemplary effort; NA = not applicable.

Many evaluations require the program to identify major strengths and weaknesses for the team before the visit occurs. Most evaluations are a combination of qualitative (interviewing, reviewing documents) and quantitative (rating programs on the previously agreed-on indicators of quality or criteria) elements, as is demonstrated in Exhibit 8.1. Occasionally there may be a concern that the program is not providing requested materials. However, most evaluators are intent on improving the program and conducting a formative evaluation (one focusing on improvement). The ideal situation is for the program to provide all requested information in order to help the evaluation team conduct a comprehensive evaluation to determine the worth of the program. This will enable the evaluators to "tell it like it is," so the program can have both accurate and appropriate recommendations and commendations for the stakeholders and audiences involved.

Conducting a Self-Evaluation. Self-evaluations often involve the work of various subcommittees made up of the various stakeholders. Generally, a subcommittee might be formed to work on each of the indicators of quality mentioned previously—for example, curriculum and instructional materials or general administration. Strengths and weaknesses for the various categories or indicators of quality can be determined and written by the stakeholders, who are more likely to know the strengths and weaknesses of the program than an outside group coming in to determine merit within a short time. Ideally, all of this information (including the strengths and weaknesses) and appropriate documents need to be forwarded to the evaluators long before the scheduled evaluation. The submission of documents several weeks before the on-site evaluation allows the evaluators time to request additional information if necessary. Stakeholders will be more likely to feel a sense of ownership in and support for the program if they are involved in the self-evaluation.

Developing Recommendations and Commendations

If the evaluation is conducted appropriately and professionally, the team will have criteria, standards, or indicators of quality on which to rate most components of the program. The indicators of quality help provide a basis for developing the recommendations and commendations. Team members should attempt to reach consensus on rating the indicators of quality that will serve as a basis for listing the recommendations and commendations. The final list of recommendations and commendations provides the primary information for the exit interview.

The exit interview should generally be conducted only by the team leader to avoid ambiguity and mixed signals to those receiving the report. It should be made clear that this is not the final report but that the exit interview is based on the preliminary report and consensus of the team involved. The forthcoming written report will serve as the official evaluation report.

Conducting the Exit Interview

A common courtesy is to involve and invite the major stakeholders and leaders associated with the evaluation process to the exit interview. However, some program administrators are reluctant to invite other staff and stakeholders for fear of negative recommendations. Generally, the evaluation will prove more useful if the major stakeholders are invited to the exit interview rather than limiting it to one key administrator. If only one key administrator attends, it is possible that this person might not understand the commendations and recommendations as well as several persons hearing the same information. Therefore, it is recommended that the major stakeholders be invited to the exit interview.

Writing a Final Report for Action

The final report should be action oriented, with a follow-up required within a thirty- to sixty-day period. A statement may be made that the administrators or program officials have thirty days to respond to each recommendation made by the evaluation team, and then the appropriate follow-up can be conducted. This action would be appropriate for programs conducted on a regional, state, or national basis. Once again, the emphasis is on making the evaluation useful, feasible, ethical, and accurate. Future funding is often determined by the follow-up on the recommendations from the evaluation report.

Conclusion

It is very important to have a clear idea of the purposes of evaluations in adult education. The Joint Committee on Standards for Educational Evaluation has helped greatly by providing standards for utility, feasibility, propriety, and accuracy of evaluations. Administrators and leaders must prepare appropriately and completely for an evaluation. Evaluation can be a critical tool in improving the program for society and for all the stakeholders. Stakeholders and consultative groups should be involved, along with the staff, in collecting and organizing the evaluation information, conducting a self-evaluation, and participating in the visit of the evaluation team. The recommendations and commendations should relate to a checklist of standards or indicators of quality. The exit interview and writing the report for action, along with follow-up activities, are very important.

Adult educators have been a leading force in developing humanistic, useful evaluations. Adult educators were among the first groups to involve stakeholders and consultative groups in an attempt to make evaluation useful to all stakeholders.

References

Joint Committee on Standards for Educational Evaluation. Standards for Evaluations of Educational Programs, Projects, and Materials. New York: McGraw-Hill, 1981.

Patton, M. Q. Practical Evaluation. Newbury Park, Calif.: Sage, 1982.

Scriven, M. Evaluation Thesaurus. (4th ed.) Newbury Park, Calif.: Sage, 1991.

Stufflebeam, D. An Interview with Daniel L. Stufflebeam. Educational Evaluation and Policy Analysis, 1980, 2 (4).

ROBERT C. MASON is professor of adult and continuing education and director of the Office of Research in Adult Continuing Education at Northern Illinois University in De Kalb.

*This chapter examines representative programs that speak to new
ways of thinking about accountability for learning.*

Satisfying Accountability Needs
with Nontraditional Methods

Sally Vernon, Lisa B. Lo Parco, Victoria J. Marsick

Limited resources, a rapidly changing economic base, ever-evolving technological dependence, and shifting demographics are increasing the need for
rapid and continual learning in our workplaces, institutions of higher education, and communities. Simultaneously, questions are being raised by diverse
sectors of our society about the appropriateness and effectiveness of what and
how we are teaching and learning, where learning takes place, how to assess
learning outcomes, and the criteria and methodology for accountability in our
learning environments (Carnevale, 1991). These concerns lead to questions
about how we, as managers and instructors, design and account for learning.

In this chapter, we first describe programs that illustrate new ways of
thinking about learning. Next, we raise questions about approaches to
accountability and illustrate them through examples from higher education,
workplace learning, and community education. We conclude by discussing
emerging concerns for adult education managers.

Examples of Alternative Education Programs

Organizations in diverse settings are turning to innovative strategies to meet
new learning needs. Their designs reflect paradigm shifts in our society that,
in turn, call for new ways of delivering and accounting for learning. The following examples illustrate these changes.

Higher Education. In an attempt to meet present and future learning
needs, institutions of higher education are implementing a variety of alternative programs in diverse settings. They are described as "alternative" because
their designs reflect the paradigm shifts that are occurring in our society and

attempt to provide a different way of offering and experiencing learning environments.

One example in higher education is degree completion programs that are offered at the baccalaureate level. These programs pair formal and informal learning that students have achieved through prior experience with new learning that is acquired through the design and delivery of the educational program. At the graduate level, many alternative programs apply the theory of course work to individual professional practice within a collaborative learning model. The delivery system of alternative programs is frequently such that students can move through the program more quickly than in more traditional programs, pursue both full-time career and educational opportunities, and play an active role in designing a program that meets their needs.

It is not unusual for alternative programs to feature partnerships with corporations or community-based organizations. The workplace literacy movement has epitomized the partnership model. Customized programs designed through such partnerships result in the attainment not only of individual participant goals but those of all of the stakeholders in the partnerships.

Workplace Learning. Corporate leaders are also initiating innovative continuous learning models, many of which occur outside of the classroom. For example, continuous improvement is associated with total quality management (TQM) and with the idea of a learning organization, popularized by Senge (1990). In TQM, everyone involved with specific products or services is linked across functions and departments to identify and satisfy customer needs. Variation in the quality of goods and services is continually measured and minimized. Workers in TQM must collaborate, communicate, and negotiate across functional boundaries; they often form teams and networks of many kinds to this end. TQM requires continual learning for continual improvement.

Learning organizations, likewise, have embedded continual learning processes. It is not enough for individuals to learn; they must share learning in such a way that the organization is also said to have learned. Training and learning in these organizations have been redefined. They are linked to business results and frequently delivered in bite-sized modules on a just-in-time basis. Employees are expected to take more initiative in solving problems. While employees are not always skilled at learning on the job, they must become self-directed learners who can identify and meet their own learning needs and learn from experience. Organizations thus provide fewer standardized, scheduled classroom activities.

Community Education. The role of community-based organizations in addressing critical learning needs has increased substantially in recent years. Programs within these agencies frequently build the capacity of the participants by improving literacy and basic skills, language acquisition, acculturation, and survival skills. Because these organizations are accessible and familiar, they are used by the community residents who most need them.

There are significant shifts in the way in which curriculum is designed and delivered in these educational programs. As program managers and faculty are recognizing that traditional methods are less than effective, they are eager to try alternatives. Learner-centered approaches are taking precedence over teacher-centered practices. Instructional materials and strategies focus on the learners' life experiences. In addition, heavy emphasis is placed on self-directed learning experiences that frequently are documented in learning contracts, which are co-designed by student and teacher.

Alternative Accountability Procedures

New designs for learning, illustrated by the previous examples, demand new approaches to accountability. We raise and answer the following questions to further examine these new approaches.

What is learning? New definitions broaden our understanding of where to look for areas of accountability.

Who are the stakeholders? Accountability means satisfying stakeholder expectations; multiple stakeholders means a broadening of the scope of accountability.

When do we need to examine accountability? Program designs now suggest a more continual process.

For what are program managers to be accountable? New designs for learning suggest a melding of new and old measures of success.

What tools and strategies are used? Accountability cannot always be measured through tests and surveys, but there is always some kind of bottom line.

Table 9.1 examines these questions as they relate to learning environments in higher education, the workplace, and community-based organizations.

Illustrations of Alternative Accountability Models

The following are alternative accountability approaches that are being tried in learning environments in higher education, workplaces, and community education that also are consistent with the data in Table 9.1.

Higher Education. The National-Louis University graduate program in adult and continuing education (in the Chicago area) is an alternative program that builds accountability methodology into the curriculum design. The program defines learning as a critical thinking process that occurs collaboratively, with the student holding significant responsibility for what is learned and how the learning takes place. The design of the program provides structure for students to acquire the content necessary to be effective adult educators; reflect on the relationship between theory and practice; gain an understanding of how individuals learn individually and in groups; and learn continually, both individually and as part of a profession or organization.

Table 9.1. Guidelines for Examining Alternative Accountability Procedures

	Community-Based Organization
What is learning?	Learning that is relevant to life and work, whether or not it results in formal accreditation; that enables people to live a full life in the community
Who are the stakeholders?	Teachers, students, administrators, government, community representatives
When does assessment occur?	Primarily as a part of formal classes
What is assessed?	Skills and knowledge acquisition of students; program reviews by funders
What tools and strategies are used?	Ranges from traditional methods such as placement and other standardized tests or teacher assessments to "authentic" assessments, such as the use of portfolios

Table 9.1 (*continued*)

Workplace	*Higher Education*
Learning that is continual, self-directed, integrated with work, and just in time for individuals and the organization as a whole	Examining the interaction of theory and practice; examining individual and group learning styles, resulting in individuals who contribute positively to their profession, the economy, and society
Trainers and training managers, employees, managers to whom employees report, customers	Students, faculty, administration, current and future employers, community groups, funding agencies, professional associations
Continual assessment, feeding into revised work, at the level of impact in the organization, not just the classroom	Continually and with a feedback loop that allows for continual change and learning
Behavioral changes, competencies, and impact on job performance; team and organizational learning	Program or course products that demonstrate an understand of the interaction between theory and practice, faculty ability to facilitate learning to understanding the relationship between theory and practice, the program curriculum, administrative and student support infrastructure, student personal and professional performance post-program
Classroom evaluation of performance has been the norm, but some new tools are 360-degree feedback and other data-based assessments that lead to performance plans, quality data on customer impact, critical incidents, and learning projects	Quantitative instruments that measure enrollment, retention, performance, and job placement data; qualitative strategies that elicit data on what and how students learn—for example, formal and informal student interviews, orientation activities and culminating seminars, advising procedures, faculty development activities, process meetings with stakeholders, learning contracts, and student products

The number of stakeholders associated with the program is expanded, and the stakes are substantially different. For example, students have an investment in the program meeting both their academic goals and their goals to participate successfully in substantially different and continually changing organizations. Employers are expecting students not only to perform well in specific jobs but to play a major role in appropriate and continual organizational change. University administrators and funding agencies have a stake in meeting shifting learning needs as well as in understanding and developing infrastructures that support alternative learning models. Communities are hoping that alternative educational programs will share in the responsibility of meeting pressing societal needs. Faculty expect to set the pace in creating new models of teaching and learning. (See the discussion of selection of group members in Chapter Five, involvement of stakeholders in Chapter Eight, and the humanistic administrator in Chapter Ten.)

Accountability procedures are continual and begin with representative stakeholders meeting to reach consensus regarding program claims, issues, and concerns. In this way, values and assumptions about the programs and goals remain surfaced and are the underpinning of accountability criteria and methodology (Guba and Lincoln, 1989).

Student accountability criteria are monitored through a series of process activities, including admissions interviews, an orientation to the program, ongoing faculty advisement, and an integrative seminar at the completion of the program. Additional methodologies include frequent informal conversations with students and faculty, exit interviews, and follow-up surveys.

Admissions interviews are conducted between potential students and faculty to determine whether a match exists between the students' learning styles and goals and the design and intent of the program. An interview guide encourages consistency across interviews and interviewers. Preliminary information is used to assess prospective student success in the program and identify discrepancies in how the program is or could be articulated.

A one-day orientation is offered for students who have been accepted into the program. The orientation provides students with detailed information about the program, the opportunity to meet and interact with members of their cohort, their first experience of the collaborative nature of program by participating primarily in group activities that highlight individual and group responsibility, a chance to reflect on and share their concerns and issues regarding the program, and an opportunity to define and articulate in writing (a personal student profile) their individual goals and the methods by which the program can meet them. In some cases, students have elected not to continue in the program after this hands-on experience.

The orientation serves as a useful accountability tool and provides a great deal of data. Faculty, who also serve as advisers, gain deeper insights into students' suitability for the program, students' intent in the program, and their potential needs for support and advisement. These data offer opportunities to identify and acquire resources appropriate to student needs and build an infra-structure that supports the program and the students.

Advisement is another point of data collection. Students are assigned an academic adviser for the tenure of their program. The adviser receives a copy of the student profile as a guide for the advisement process. The role of the adviser is to follow student academic progress, gauge the degree to which the program is addressing the goals of the student, and identify resources that support successful completion of the program. Advisement is a source of continuing feedback to faculty regarding the effectiveness of the program. The feedback also poses possibilities for alternatives to existing procedures and additional program or faculty development activities that would enhance the current program.

A culminating integrative seminar is integral to program accountability methodology. The curriculum for this course was developed by a team of full- and part-time faculty members who taught frequently in the program and saw its potential for benefiting students and accountability procedures. The purpose of the course is to assist students in recognizing the learning that occurred for them during the program; assessing individual learning styles that led to their success in the program; identifying which aspects or activities of the program design were most helpful to them; and, finally, developing a continual learning plan and the resources that they would require to accomplish the plan. The data that surface during this course are essential to faculty assessment of program strengths and needed enhancements.

Ongoing faculty and adviser meetings are conducted routinely and are structured to share and document accountability data obtained from each of these methodologies, discuss and analyze the implications of the data on the program, brainstorm on possible program enhancements, identify stakeholders who should be involved in decision making and implementation, incorporate the changes, and continue the feedback process.

The use of learning contracts is another alternative measure of student learning. As testing is not used in the program, learning contracts allow students to identify products that document their understanding of the content of each course that are consistent with their interests and goals and to demonstrate their understanding of the implications of the learning on their practice. Students also propose the weighting of their work in grade assignments and, in some cases, the people who should be involved in the assessment process. Members of the cohort, employers, or representatives of relevant agencies might be included in evaluating student work. The learning contract is developed and negotiated with the instructor of record by the third week of each course. Changes in the contract are negotiated and recorded as appropriate and necessary. (See the discussion of participatory research in Chapter Two and active learner participation in staff development in Chapter Six.)

Traditional quantitative accountability data are also collected, including data on enrollment, retention, and career advancement. Follow-up surveys, exit interviews, and institutional sources are used to collect this type of information. (See the definition of accountability in Chapter One and the discussion of taxpayer scrutiny in Chapter Five.)

The role of full- and part-time faculty in this type of learning model is different from that in traditional programs. Rather than acting primarily as teachers, they provide guidance through the self-directed learning process; they highlight not only their own expertise and knowledge base but also those of the students, and they facilitate both individual and group learning and serve as mentors and advocates for their students. In addition, they are partners with other stakeholders in curriculum and program development and are active participants in the accountability process.

Workplace Learning Programs. Johnsonville Foods, Granite Rock, and Manulife Financial are considered to be in the vanguard in establishing new ways of thinking about and conducting learning in the corporate environment (Watkins and Marsick, 1993). While they adhere to the traditional belief that learning must be linked to business results, they have made the shift from a reliance on standardized, scheduled classroom activities to an understanding that people need to learn how to learn on the job and often in teams.

Johnsonville Foods, for example, has moved beyond the belief that learning has to be directly related to individual performance to activities that help people develop a learning habit. The company sets aside funds that each employee can spend in any way he or she wishes: "The learning experience doesn't have to be work related, but it does have to encourage the person to think" (Honold, 1991, p. 57).

An additional change that has occurred in the Granite Rock learning model is that the "student" population has been extended to include more people than just the workers or managers of Granite Rock. Rather, Granite Rock perceives a need for and the reality of learning about the organization extending beyond the boundaries of the organization, that is, to the customer. For example, at Granite Rock, "One recent session [on chemical additives] . . . attracted more than 100 customers and cost about $6000. . . . 'I can blow $6,000 like that on a messed up job'" (Case, 1992, p. 66, italics in original). Granite Rock has redefined not only its "student" but also the costs and benefits of doing so.

Dramatic shifts in how teaching and learning take place in organizations that see continual learning as vital to their survival are driving an equally dramatic change in how and when people are held accountable for results. For example, accountability cannot wait for performance evaluation deadlines if people are to learn continually. In Granite Rock, employees develop individual professional development plans with their supervisors. They map work and learning goals, identify formal and informal strategies to reach these goals, and set target dates. Every quarter they review their progress. Rosow and Zager (1988) describe similar efforts by other organizations as "learning by objectives" (p. 57). Objectives are identified along with performance targets in clear, measurable terms and are revised during the year as needed. This practice, however, is not yet the norm for groups other than managerial, professional, and technical employees. (See the description of learning community programs in Chapter One.)

Ongoing feedback is perceived as a critical assessment strategy at Manulife Financial. It has created a continual learning center, made assessment a starting point in development planning through a leadership profile, and created a 360-degree feedback tool (LaLonde-Bard, 1992). This approach leads to one-to-one coaching, individual development plans, and strategic assignments to develop a manager's potential. Rosow and Zager (1988) describe technically oriented continual learning centers "whereby a group of employees who operate similar equipment come together to learn from one another how to achieve higher performance from their equipment" (p. 67). Feedback and continual sharing of information are central to this design. The organization plays a role in accountability in these designs, but individuals also assume responsibility for their own learning and that of others.

Trainers and learners likewise seek new ways of measuring behavioral changes, competencies, and impact on job performance. Leading-edge companies, according to Rosow and Zager (1988), begin with clear statements of objectives that tie training results to business strategy. Managers are accountable for training choices, but they share accountability with human resource specialists and other stakeholders, including, at times, those who will be trained. A program at one of Tennessee Eastman's manufacturing plants illustrates the way in which accountability for training is ensured: a team approach to decision making, agreed-on objectives tied to work performance, detailed job and task analysis to focus training content, and measurement of performance against targets during and after training.

Required skills are not always easy to measure, which makes accountability all the more difficult. It is more difficult, for example, to measure self-confidence or motivation to learn than to measure work processing or machine assembly skills. An American Society for Training and Development study (Carnevale, 1991) identified basic skills for the new economy, many of which illustrate this problem: learning how to learn; reading, writing and computation; speaking and listening; problem solving and creativity; self-esteem, motivation and goal setting; personal and career development; group effectiveness; and influencing skills. These skills are the foundation for other tasks; they look different in different people; and they may be hidden because their mastery is behind success in other observable skills.

To sum up, a push toward continual learning has altered who is held accountable for what in the workplace. In the industrial era, supervisors were charged with being their brothers' keepers. In the knowledge era, employees must become their own keepers by taking responsibility for their learning. Employees must also learn from one another and share their gains so that the organization also learns. Accountability is not done unto employees; employees take the initiative, in cooperation with the organization, to ensure, measure, and improve results.

In their alternative learning model, Johnsonville Foods has provided leadership regarding the role of trainers. Their training department has become the member development department. Trainers are now serving as learning consultants to line managers so that they can assist employees in becoming self-directed learners who can identify and meet their own learning needs and who can learn from experience.

Community Development and Education. The Town Mandated Adult Program (TMAP) and City Adult Learning Center (CALC) are two community-based programs with contrasting approaches to answering the five questions noted earlier. These programs depict the changing paradigms in teaching and learning. They also illustrate how assessment of both takes place and accountability to all of the stakeholders is upheld. While both programs provide instruction for adults that focuses on improving basic skills in reading, writing, or computation, their teaching and learning strategies and visions of effective accountability procedures are strikingly different.

TMAP has met with much skepticism from community leaders since its inception. Community leaders wonder whether and why such a wealthy, influential community as Town has a literacy problem. In fact, many Town officials have been heard to say, "We don't have any illiterate people living here in Town." As a result, TMAP is being reluctantly funded by the board of education, with supplemental funding coming from state and federal governments.

Adult students are taught in the evening in a traditional classroom at Town High School, using primarily lecture formats. Most of the teachers come from the local secondary and elementary schools and do not receive formal training in adult education. Classroom materials, recommended by the board of education, are academically based and not particularly relevant to jobs or life.

Because politicians, legislators, policy makers, and funders of the program define adult basic education as a set of academic skills, the expected student outcome is mastery of a set of skills. Standardized tests are administered at the beginning and the end of the program to measure "skills acquisition" and most frequently within the formal classroom environment.

An alternative approach is offered by CALC, which offers adult basic education programs regionally, focusing on those geographic areas with the greatest need. It is administered by the local community college system, and instruction is offered in libraries, religious organizations, and other community-based agencies. A strong partnership with the corporate sector exists. In fact, many of City's major companies and small businesses support CALC with both financial and human resources. (See the discussion of external resources in Chapter One, partnerships with movers in Chapter Two, and adequate resources in Chapter Three.)

CALC is regarded as an alternative and progressive program by the local education community because of the design of its curriculum and instruction and program and student evaluation. Teachers who are attracted to the center are also perceived as nontraditional in philosophy and practice.

The characteristics that give the program its "alternative" image are a strong learner-centered approach and a holistic language philosophy in its individualized and small-group instruction. Whole language is based on the learner's life experience and knowledge while learning to read, write, and speak English and do arithmetic. Educational materials are connected to learner goals and have real-life meaning. The intent of this curriculum design is to enhance the learner's self-concept and esteem by establishing him or her as a partner in the learner project and process.

CALC's approach to program accountability is nontraditional and based on a portfolio assessment of learner affective and cognitive outcomes. Academic accomplishment or learning can range from improved self-esteem, to job placement, to good citizenship. The partnership between the instructor and learner extends to the assessment process. They collaborate in the assessment design and materials, and they frequently provide self-reports and peer reports to support the learning that has transpired in the program. In this way, an alternative assessment that is "program-centered and student-centered" (Wolfe, 1989) is an integral part of the CALC model.

The vehicle for alternative assessment is a portfolio developed by the student and used by both the student and the teacher to establish a contract that defines learning goals that are consistent with student needs, serve as a journal to record student progress toward the goals, and provide samples of student work or work done in collaboration with their peers. Teachers incorporate the portfolio into the curriculum in order to attend to diverse community education program models, students' individual learning styles and goals, and unique learning contexts.

New Roles and Emerging Concerns

This chapter has provided examples of alternative programs and accountability procedures and has illustrated shifts in views of learning across diverse settings. Accountability is being redefined by those who want a closer relationship to the immediate customer/learner/stakeholder. This requires reorientation of those who serve the customers and provide learning opportunities. A broad range of "customers" play a pivotal role in ensuring that the right objectives are established and that they are indeed satisfied by the results.

Accountability in hierarchical settings often meant someone sitting in judgment on everyone else. Now, everyone is expected to hold himself or herself accountable for results. For people on both sides of the hierarchical fence, this reversal of expectations requires a new way of thinking about power and responsibility.

Accountability demands better strategies for measuring success at a time when we are not yet clear about the indicators for success, especially with respect to some of the "softer" skills of customer service, personal capabilities, and interpersonal and group skills. This is also true for new definitions of learning that are not oriented primarily to delivery of services to passive students and that go beyond changes in behaviors (to include feelings, attitudes, and new ways of thinking.) Finally, accountability goes beyond individual gains to include learning for groups, organizations, and communities.

These changes in how learning is defined and managed are driving changes in roles demanded of managers and educators across learning environments. Instead of just teaching, adult educators are serving as advocates within their institutions for alternative models of teaching and learning and infrastructures that will support them. They act as project managers by being aware of the need for and cultivating a system for teaching and learning rather than just a course or curriculum. The increase in partnership programs and stakeholders in the educational process necessitates educators' serving as negotiators and collaborators rather than autonomous entities in a classroom. As organizations and programs assume responsibility for the whole person, educators are managing the multiple linkages that are required to nurture the affective, familial, and cognitive development of their customers or students.

Clearly, there is a need to provide similar development opportunities for managers and educators to help them meet new challenges; to begin to view new or alternative models for learning and accountability as authentic; and to perceive multiple methodologies (that is, quantitative and qualitative accountability strategies) as effective. There is a need to continue to try innovation in learning and accountability as frequently as is necessary to address continual learning needs.

References

Carnevale, A. P. America and the New Economy: How New Competitive Standards Are Radically Changing American Workplaces. San Francisco: Jossey-Bass, 1991.

Case, J. "The Change Masters." Inc., March 1992, pp. 57–70.

Guba, E. G., and Lincoln, Y. S. Fourth Generation Evaluation. Newbury Park, Calif.: Sage, 1989.

Honold, L. "The Power of Learning at Johnsonville Foods." Training, 1991, 28 (4), 55–58.

LaLonde-Bard, J. "Learning Strategies for Executives." Presentation at The Learning Organization: Strategies to Make it Happen conference of the Canadian Human Resources Planning Society, Toronto, Nov. 1992.

Rosow, J. M., and Zager, R. Training—The Competitive Edge: Introducing New Technology into the Workplace. San Francisco: Jossey-Bass, 1988.

Senge, P. The Fifth Discipline: The Art and Practice of the Learning Organization. New York: Doubleday, 1990.

Watkins, K. E., and Marsick, V. J. Sculpting the Learning Organization: Lessons in the Art and Science of Systemic Change. San Francisco: Jossey-Bass, 1993.

Wolfe, M. "Rethinking Assessment: Issues to Consider." Information Update, Literacy Assistance Center, Sept. 6, 1989.

SALLY VERNON is faculty chair and program director, Department of Adult and Continuing Education, National-Louis University.

LISA B. LO PARCO is adjunct assistant professor of adult and continuing education, Teachers College, Columbia University.

VICTORIA J. MARSICK is associate professor of adult and continuing education, Teachers College, Columbia University.

This chapter describes seven types of administrators whose management and leadership practices and approaches to instruction are rooted in liberal, behaviorist, progressive, humanist, radical, transformationalist, and cognitivist philosophies.

Putting Adult Education Philosophies into Practice

Patricia Mulcrone

How can the adult and continuing education administrator employ new strategies to fulfill changing roles in a context of day-to-day decision making and problem solving? In answer to this question, this chapter will identify philosophies (and forces, categories, or theories); extrapolate the effects of philosophies on management, leadership, and instruction; and identify administrative issues. The chapter will also summarize the contributions of previous chapters and comment on the administrative literature.

Influence of Philosophies on Administrative Practice

How do philosophies influence the adult and continuing education administrator? Philosophies can influence one's selection of compatible professional positions, preferred relationships with learners, and relationships with internal and external resources. They can influence formulation of program mission, approaches to program planning, staff management, curriculum and instructional development, budgeting and financing, and evaluation of research. Philosophies also influence the role the learner takes in learning, the instructional role the teacher adopts, and the assessment methods staff use (Elias and Merriam, 1980).

Philosophies, Forces, Categories, and Theories

Elias and Merriam (1980) identify six philosophies: liberal, progressive, behaviorist, humanistic, radical, and analytical. Zinn (1983) identifies five of the same philosophies, excluding the analytical. Boucouvalas (1983) cites the first three forces as psychoanalytical, behaviorist, and humanistic, followed by transpersonal psychology as a fourth force. Merriam (1988) refers to the three "most common categories of learning theories [as] behaviorism, humanism, and cognitivism" (p. 5). One other philosophy indicated in the literature is the transformationalist.

How does one discern one's administrative philosophy? Zinn's (1983) "Philosophy of Adult Education Inventory," which is self-administered, scored, and interpreted, identifies to what degree an adult educator subscribes to each of five philosophies: liberal, behaviorist, progressive, humanistic, and radical. Those who take the test are often surprised that their scores indicate a particular basic philosophy or an eclectic combination of two or three philosophies.

Another way to determine one's philosophy is to build a framework for a personal philosophy of adult education by responding to fundamental questions about the nature of adult education. These questions have evolved from a review of historical highlights of American adult education that indicate roles played by particular institutions or providers, individual adult educators, acts of legislation, organizations, publications, and movements (Grattan, 1959; Knowles, 1977; Elias and Merriam, 1980; Rippa, 1988):

What are the purposes (goals and objectives) of adult education?
What should be the content or subject matter of adult education? Should the content include values?
Who should learn? Who should teach?
Where (in which settings) should adult education be taught?
Who should pay for adult education? How should adult education be funded? Should there be any limits on services?

Effects on Management, Leadership, and Instruction

How would the adult and continuing education administrator holding these various philosophies approach management and leadership roles? How would the administration view instruction and interact with instructors? (See the discussion of management of multiple grants in Chapter Three, the adult educator as manager of groups in Chapter Five, and management functions in Chapter Seven.)

Liberal. The liberal adult education administrator might serve as a mentor or colleague to faculty and staff but not as a strict manager or controller. This type of administrator would appear to faculty to be a peer or perhaps even a sage but would seldom require strict observance of institutional norms. If this administrator held a department chair position, it would likely be rotated in some years to other faculty members. This administrator might support systems of shared governance (between administration and faculty) but probably not participatory governance (inclusive of nonprofessional staff).

The liberal adult education administrator would likely serve as a model of cultural refinement; he or she would support the humanities, fine arts programs, moral or spiritual studies, great books reading and discussion series, and scholarship programs. This type of administrator would encourage faculty exchanges with other institutions, sister cities projects, coordinated studies, study abroad, and philosophical or historical research. The liberal administrator would likely hire instructors who treat curriculum as a subject matter expert and who prefer autonomy in course design.

Behaviorist. The behaviorist adult education administrator would have definite (often written) policies, procedures, and directives and would expect faculty and staff to follow his or her hierarchical lead in a defined system of protocol. This type of administrator would expect forms of rationale with supporting data for all staff requests. This administrator would likely rate a majority of faculty and staff on performance scales according to the bell-shaped curve.

This administrator would likely favor performance contracts or written staff goals followed by reports of accomplishments. He or she would likely employ staff control strategies, require near-perfect products, take actual (or mental) staff attendance at meetings, note committee assignments and roles, and enforce institutional policies. The behaviorist administrator would probably greatly value the master budget as a quantitative tool, as described by Ericksen in Chapter Four. The "Matrix of Administrative Technologies and Management Functions," included by Porter in Chapter Seven (see Table 7.1), would appeal to the behaviorist administrator's need for structure, direction, and organization.

The behaviorist adult education administrator would probably expect a curriculum with detailed course outlines showing objectives and precise measures of student progress and transition. This type of administrator would be most comfortable with all types of quantitative student testing, including placement, diagnostic achievement, and predictive testing. The behaviorist administrator would probably have less difficulty than other administrators with defining goals, objectives, and activities, as explained by Brewer in Chapter Three, and would be able to write objectives that call for short-term, specific, and realistic expressions. This administrator would be able to work with residential adult communities, trainers, personnel or human resource developers in business, or the military establishment to accommodate and measure specific goals.

Progressive. The progressive adult education administrator would be a great organization person and probably would have a plan for cooperation with federal, state, and local agencies. This type of administrator would readily attend meetings of outside agencies, summarize adult education trends, and share information with staff. This administrator would probably serve in the role of informed leader and community contributor.

In relation to staff, the progressive administrator would be concerned with systems with which to organize work, explain projects, delegate duties, meet deadlines, communicate effectively, and update field information. This administrator would probably quickly become expert at "doing more with less," take on more responsibilities, pool monetary resources, utilize group expertise, use team experiences, and resolve conflicts. The administrator might organize or attend a roundtable or advisory council to share approaches to common problems. He or she would probably be very cooperative in preparation for an adult education program evaluation, as described by Mason in Chapter Eight.

The progressive adult education administrator would be most comfortable with curriculum that enhances the transmission of societal and cultural values. This type of administrator would be likely to respond, as Brewer describes in Chapter Three, to federal solicited grants for dropout prevention, migrant education, and retention of dislocated workers. He or she would favor instructional sequences that empower the disadvantaged, encourage acculturation of immigrants, and solve community problems. This administrator would likely conduct needs assessments of learner needs, interests, and experiences as a common way to design curriculum. He or she would likely accept the aspects of a strong in-service program identified by Terdy in Chapter Six.

Humanistic. The humanistic adult education administrator might have difficulty being a strict administrator because human relationships are very important for his or her interpretation and implementation of institutional policies and procedures. This type of administrator (or manager) would be a good ally, supporter, and friend of the adult education unit's faculty and staff because creation of a "family" atmosphere, trust, and mutual support are so important to him or her. This administrator would agree with Charuhas, who recommends in Chapter Five that those who will be stakeholders in a group's results should help select the group's members. As stressed by Mason in Chapter Eight, this administrator would be very comfortable with involving stakeholders in the entire evaluation process. Similarly, this administrator would agree with Vernon, Lo Parco, and Marsick, who state in Chapter Nine that "accountability means satisfying stakeholder expectations."

The humanistic administrator would involve the stakeholders in the teaching-learning exchange. Consistent with the view of Vernon, Lo Parco, and Marsick in Chapter Nine, the humanistic administrator (or manager) would define learning as continual, self-directed, integrated, and relevant to life. This administrator would favor any curriculum that promotes individual students' personal growth, career development, motivation and self-direction, freedom and autonomy, and self-actualization. This type of administrator would agree with Norland (1991) regarding student assessment in stating that students "should be consulted when strategies are designed, selected, modified, or eliminated" (p. 24).

The humanistic administrator would encourage instructors to work in teams or clusters and to involve students in course planning, individual assignments and projects, evaluation, and grading of student progress. The teacher as mentor and guide and promoter of more flexible learning driven by the learner, as addressed by Porter in Chapter Seven, is consistent with the humanist philosophy. As Terdy emphasizes in Chapter Six, the humanistic administrator would actively involve participants in design and delivery of preservice and in-service programs and literacy providers groups.

Radical. Perhaps a better designation than radical adult education administrator might be "chief change agent." This type of administrator would likely be the director of a community-based agency and could find it difficult to "play the game" to apply for, receive, and retain funding from established agencies. This administrator could consciously or unconsciously view faculty and staff in terms of dichotomies: urban and suburban, minority and majority, hegemonic and counterhegemonic. To this administrator, faculty and staff would need to be political-social activists who help solve rather than simply identify community problems and bring about conscientization and societal change.

The radical administrator might not manage an adult program for compulsory schooling but would favor education for political liberation, popular education, and health education. More likely would be the administrator's use of a community advisory group to determine true instructional needs. This administrator would likely support programs for the disadvantaged, urban literacy, or Third World literacy.

This administrator would expect instructors (really coordinators) to treat their students as liberated, self-motivated equals who determine learning directions. The administrator would expect instructors to use methods that emphasize open dialogue, group discussion, and problem-posing education (critical investigation of social issues).

Transformationalist. In a more highly developed model of humanistic (or possibly radical) education, one could evolve into a transformationalist adult education administrator. This administrator might have difficulty focusing on routine or practical concerns, especially budgeting or record-keeping needs.

This type of administrator would probably be excellent at designing intensive projects for faculty sabbaticals or leading faculty or staff in phenomenological research studies (concerning the root of experience, relations and connections among aspects of knowledge, consciousness, and the suspension of judgment). As Heaney suggests in Chapter Two, the transformationalist administrator could promote a vision of education that deepens understanding of contemporary issues to help decide social and political directions. The administrator could facilitate a model of participatory program evaluation and encourage staff and learners to identify barriers to improvement.

With the transformationalist philosophy, the administrator would encourage serious personal reflection and self-examination so that the instructor or student would transcend personal views to reach a newer and higher level of self-actualization. The Action Research Professional Development Program (related to Mezirow's study), which is cited by Terdy in Chapter Six and depicts the instructor acting as a reflective researcher, could be viewed as transformationalist.

This administrator would challenge cultural assumptions and employ instructional methods that encourage adults to identify real problems, recognize dependent roles and relationships, and overcome dependencies. As Heaney suggests in Chapter Two, students would reflect on their experience and turn it into knowledge that becomes a power to act. With increasing competence and self-confidence, students would assume new roles and be further integrated into society.

Cognitivist. The cognitivist adult education administrator would likely excel at aspects of the job that involved leading staff in new directions, designing in-service or train-the-trainer programs, or creating systems. The design of systems for decision making, task assignments, management responsibility, and problem solving, as described by Charuhas in Chapter Five, would be a comfortable activity for the cognitivist. Adept at analysis of others' thoughts, this type of administrator could probably enhance the personal growth of staff, providing them with feedback.

The cognitivist administrator could encourage creativity by seeing most things as drafts in a constant state of becoming; however, this might frustrate staff members who need closure. The break-even analysis aspect of budgets and multidimensional budgeting, as explained by Ericksen in Chapter Four, would be activities suited to the cognitivist, who is adept in analytical thinking.

The cognitivist administrator would encourage or facilitate linear or circular needs assessments, instructors' emphasis of foundation skills (learning how to learn), identification and matching of student and teacher learning styles, and collaborative learning (Smith, 1982; Smith and Associates, 1990). This type of administrator would direct the design or delivery of instruction in terms of levels of formal operations of cognition, concept formation and attainment, discovery learning, and learning aids such as cognitive mapping, advance organizers (key course concepts or organizing principles), and subsumers (lower-order concepts). This administrator would also be comfortable with inventories, knowledge coding systems, participation training (for different roles in any learning group), and case studies.

Future Directions Related to Administrative Issues

Regardless of personal philosophy, the adult and continuing education administrator must continue to address issues. In addition to the philosophies described in this chapter, another philosophy that has gained recent acceptance is total quality management (TQM). TQM combines elements of other philosophies. The TQM focus on enabling, supporting, and assisting students in an atmosphere of trust is consistent with humanism. The administrator's acting as a coach and facilitator for staff on teams is also humanistic. The structure of staff support and the implementation of TQM in corporate training could suggest behaviorism. Also, the collective responsibility, decentralized controls, and participatory decision making, as described by Heaney in Chapter Two, could be elements of radicalism. Thus, an issue is the compatibility of TQM with other philosophies and its utility in adult education settings.

Appropriate methods of marketing for education (Draves, 1990; Havlicek, 1990) will continue to be an issue. Decentralization will persist as an administrative issue and direction, particularly in continuing education. Simerly (1990) alludes to the basic changes experienced by organizations as the decentralization of services resulting in sharing of power and decision making. Baden (1991) addresses the issue of decentralization of continuing education on many college campuses across the nation; he calls for leadership in answering questions of continuing education power interests and student access to quality.

More collaborative and cooperative instructional approaches will be promoted by the critical literacy movement, which encourages faculty to stress critical thinking, problem solving, and decision making. Instructors will experiment more with approaches that transfer the locus of control from them to students for course planning, instructional delivery, student testing, and grading. Instructors will accept more student papers in the form of major papers, year-long or major-long personal inquiries, real-life research symposia, portfolios, and other formats.

The direction of student assessment will need to be linked more with academic skills testing, course placement, demonstration of skills acquisition and proficiency, and curriculum design. Assessment methods and tools will need to be more explicit as stakeholders look more to demonstrated student progress and educational guarantees.

Perhaps one of the most important administrative issues is a lack of leadership today. Simerly (quoted in "Top Leadership Skills . . . ," 1991) identifies the abilities to deal with or manage ambiguity, simultaneity, conflict, transformational leadership, marketing, computer technology, financial planning, decentralized decision making, a dynamic organizational culture, and strategic planning. Some researchers, including Spikes (1991), indicate the need to prepare new leaders through attention to educational standards, professional values, ethics, and behavior. Important for consideration is attention to leadership style and the necessity for flexibility, change in style, and opportunities for leadership development.

Summary and Conclusions

Preceding chapters have analyzed the role of the adult education administrator today in terms of internal and external resources; educational, social, and political issues; funding sources and grant documents; budgets; program development; staff development; technology; monitoring and evaluation; and accountability. In these contexts the adult education administrator has utilized expected knowledge and skills, but he or she has also exercised some skills occasionally, to a lesser degree, or in different settings. In more current practice, perhaps these can be called *enhanced skills*. Authors of previous chapters have demonstrated that administrators need enhanced skills that include the following:

Utilizing internal and external resources and developing proficiencies in needs analyses and staffing for other settings (Mulcrone, Chapter One)

Dealing with crucial educational, social, and political issues for collective problem posing, strategy building, and action (Heaney, Chapter Two)

Refining grants management skills through preparing multiple proposals or applications to public and private agencies, and managing and administering projects (Brewer, Chapter Three)

Adopting other approaches to budgeting, such as the flexible budget or the multidimensional budget, for complex adult education environments (Ericksen, Chapter Four)

Working with unilateral and multilateral groups to build strong relationships, design systems for decision making, manage responsibility, and solve problems (Charuhas, Chapter Five)

Recruiting new faculty or staff through preservice activities and building a community of teachers and learners through treating staff development as a focused, flexible, continuing process that is interrelated with adult education programs (Terdy, Chapter Six)

Using technology to best advantage to redefine modes of instruction, access on-line research tools, facilitate and empower staff (Porter, Chapter Seven)

Preparing for evaluation and utilizing evaluation as a humanistic tool for program improvement (Mason, Chapter Eight)

Addressing accountability for groups, organizations, and communities through nontraditional means and redefining power and responsibility (Vernon, Lo Parco, and Marsick, Chapter Nine)

Recognizing the effects of adult education philosophies on administrative practice and blending philosophies or developing new ones (Mulcrone, Chapter Ten)

Reviewing the sources cited by the eleven authors of this sourcebook, one can determine the types of available materials and areas in which adult education administration needs further written discussion. Relatively few citations were from expected sources: *Adult Learning, Continuing Higher Education,* general books on adult education (mostly from 1960–1980 except for several from 1989–1992), *Leadership Abstracts, Innovation Abstracts,* and *New Directions* sourcebooks. Several citations were from dissertations, national special projects and directories, and general circulation periodicals (*Inc., Business Week, On Campus, Training, Information Update,* and so on).

Interestingly, a number unpublished works or reports, conference papers and presentations, and ERIC documents were cited, which leads one to conclude that administrators are seeking the most relevant, up-to-date information from their colleagues. It is encouraging that while authors cited a number of books specifically on administration, management, leadership, training, or grantsmanship, two-thirds of them were published after 1987.

Finally, the most unexpected and telling observation was the variety and number of special-interest journals that were cited (for example, *Journal of American Speech and Hearing Association; Journal of College Science Teaching; Journal of Physical Education, Recreation, and Dance; Journal of Accountancy; Electronic Learning*). The clear message is that professional groups with affiliations related to adult education are giving a fair amount of attention to administrative, management, and leadership issues and directions. Those of us who call ourselves adult educators, especially adult and continuing education administrators, could give the subject more attention as well.

References

Baden, C. "Continuing Higher Education: Reflections on Leadership and Success." *Journal of Continuing Higher Education,* 1991, *39* (1), 23–25.

Boucouvalas, M. "Social Transformation, Lifelong Learning, and the Fourth Force—Transpersonal Psychology." *Lifelong Learning: The Adult Years,* 1983, *6* (7), 6–9.

Draves, W. A. "Marketing Issues of the 1990s." *Adult Learning,* 1990, *2* (1), 6.

Elias, J. L., and Merriam, S. B. *Philosophical Foundations of Adult Education.* Huntington, N.Y.: Krieger, 1980.

Grattan, C. H. *American Ideas About Adult Education, 1710–1951.* New York: Teachers College, Columbia University, 1959.

Havlicek, C. "Demystifying Database Marketing." *Adult Learning,* 1990, *2* (1), 13–15.

Knowles, M. S. *A History of the Adult Education Movement in the United States.* Huntington, N.Y.: Krieger, 1977.

Merriam, S. B. "Finding Your Way Through the Maze: A Guide to the Literature on Adult Learning." *Lifelong Learning: An Omnibus of Practice and Research,* 1988, *11* (6), 4–7.

Norland, E. "Student Assessment: Same Recipe, New Pan." *Adult Learning,* 1991, *3* (3), 24–25.

Rippa, S. A. *Education in a Free Society.* (6th ed.) New York: Longman, 1988.

Simerly, R. G. "Stratonomics Developing New Leadership Skills." *Adult Learning,* 1990, *1* (4), 19–22.

Smith, R. M. *Learning How to Learn.* New York: Cambridge, 1982.

Smith, R. M., and Associates. *Learning to Learn Across the Life Span.* San Francisco: Jossey-Bass, 1990.

Spikes, W. F. "Transforming the Leadership Paradigm." *Adult Learning,* 1991, *3* (3), 4.

"Top Leadership Skills Named for Continuing Educators in the '90s." *Adult and Continuing Educators Today,* 1991, *21* (45), 1.

Zinn, L. M. "Philosophy of Adult Education Inventory." Unpublished doctoral dissertation, Florida State University, Tallahassee, 1983.

PATRICIA MULCRONE *is professor and chair of the Adult Educational Development Department at William Rainey Harper College, Palatine, Illinois. She has also served as an adult education instructor, presenter, and professional association officer.*

INDEX

Ordering Information

NEW DIRECTIONS FOR ADULT AND CONTINUING EDUCATION is a series of paperback books that explores issues of common interest to instructors, administrators, counselors, and policy makers in a broad range of adult and continuing education settings—such as colleges and universities, extension programs, businesses, the military, prisons, libraries, and museums. Books in the series are published quarterly in Spring, Summer, Fall, and Winter and are available for purchase by subscription and individually.

SUBSCRIPTIONS for 1993 cost $47.00 for individuals (a savings of 25 percent over single-copy prices) and $62.00 for institutions, agencies, and libraries. Please do not send institutional checks for personal subscriptions. Standing orders are accepted.

SINGLE COPIES cost $15.95 when payment accompanies order. (California, New Jersey, New York, and Washington, D.C., residents please include appropriate sales tax.) Billed orders will be charged postage and handling.

DISCOUNTS FOR QUANTITY ORDERS are available. Please write to the address below for information.

ALL ORDERS must include either the name of an individual or an official purchase order number. Please submit your order as follows:
  Subscriptions: specify series and year subscription is to begin
  Single copies: include individual title code (such as CE1)

MAIL ALL ORDERS TO:
  Jossey-Bass Publishers
  350 Sansome Street
  San Francisco, California 94104-1342

FOR SINGLE-COPY SALES OUTSIDE OF THE UNITED STATES CONTACT:
  Maxwell Macmillan International Publishing Group
  866 Third Avenue
  New York, New York 10022

FOR SUBSCRIPTION SALES OUTSIDE OF THE UNITED STATES, contact any international subscription agency or Jossey-Bass directly.